SECRET
CHICAGO

SECRET CHICAGO

The Unique Guidebook to Chicago's Hidden Sites, Sounds, & Tastes

Revised Edition

Sam Weller

WITH PHOTOGRAPHS BY
Linda Rutenberg

ECW PRESS

The publication of *Secret Chicago* has been generously supported by the Canada Council, the Ontario Arts Council, and the Government of Canada through the Book Publishing Industry Development Program. Canadä

NATIONAL LIBRARY OF CANADA CATALOGUING IN PUBLICATION DATA

Weller, Sam, 1967-
Secret Chicago: the unique guidebook to Chicago's hidden sites, sounds & tastes
Rev. ed.
Includes index.
ISBN 1-55022-493-X
I. Chicago (Ill.) – Guidebooks. II. Title.
F548.18.W44 2002   917.73'110444   C2001-903595-0

Original series design: Paul Davies, ECW Type and Art, Oakville, Ontario.
Series editor: Laura Byrne Paquet.
Typesetting: Martel *en-tête*.
Imaging and cover: Guylaine Régimbald – SOLO DESIGN.
Printed by University of Toronto Press.

Distributed in Canada by Stewart House Publishing Inc.,
290 North Queen Street, Suite 210, Etobicoke, Ontario M9C 5K4.

Distributed in the United States by Independent Publishers Group,
814 North Franklin Street, Chicago, Illinois 60610.

Published by ECW PRESS
2120 Queen Street East, Suite 200, Toronto, Ontario M4E 1E2.

ecwpress.com

PRINTED AND BOUND IN CANADA

TABLE OF CONTENTS

INTRODUCTION

Chicago is a paradoxical city. It's tough and it's tender. It's crude yet sophisticated. This travel guide looks to capture both sides of that character. The city is a straight-shooting, no b.s. kind of town. And in that spirit, this guide sets out to show you all facets of this great metropolis, without glazing over and romanticizing it like other travel guides have done.

Writer Nelson Algren once said Chicago was like a beautiful woman with a broken nose. Those guides don't tell you about that broken nose. This one does. Why? Because in order to truly understand Chicago, and to experience it and love it like you've lived in it forever, you have to appreciate both sides of the paradox.

What this means is that you can't just visit the Art Institute of Chicago or shop at the glitzy Water Tower Place mall and walk away with a feel for the city. In fact, I'll warn you when you venture into the realm of the tourist and direct you instead to the leafy neighborhoods and the tiny ma and pa stores. This is how you will get to know our city. I'll beckon you, for example, to a dark and smoky blues club where the daughter of a blues legend wails well past the witching hour — singing to a small crowd of neighborhood regulars. I'll invite you to the far Southwest Side to sample the garlic kielbasa at a Polish deli, and afterwards to wander to a nearby all-night bowling alley with 80 lanes. I'll open the door to a vegetarian restaurant where you can sit on a screened-in porch as the nearby elevated train rumbles by overhead. I'll take you to the best place for punk rock, and to the place the punk rockers get their tattoos.

This guide will also save you money with a naughty tip on how to cheat the tollbooths on the local expressways, and with clear-cut advice on how the city's train system operates. I'll direct you to one of the most expensive hotel suites in town, and I'll show you how to lodge comfortably for a whole week for little more than $100. It takes a local to know these things, and you have a local as your guide. Leaf through this book, choose a topic, and explore. Before long, you'll be a local too.

HOW TO USE
SECRET CHICAGO

This book is arranged alphabetically, by subject. If you're a jazz aficionado, flip to "Secret Jazz"; if you're an architecture enthusiast, turn to "Secret Architecture." Craving a sweet from a far-off land? Go to "Secret Ethnic Bakeries." Want to shoot a game of pool in a real old-fashioned pool hall? Go to . . . well, you get the point.

With every location, I've provided a phone number and an address. Recently, the city of Chicago and its surrounding suburbs have gone bonkers over area codes, so this book gives them with every telephone number. And while the majority of the listings stick to sweet home Chicago, there are a few irresistible treats just on the outskirts. I don't list hours of operation, driving directions, or prices unless there's something unique about them. Call ahead to find all of this out — and, admittedly, to ensure that a place is still in operation. Chicago is in the midst of a gentrification storm and the smaller businesses, unfortunately, sometimes just curl up and die. Still, this handy-dandy little book is newly revised and the utmost care has been taken to ensure that all the businesses listed within were up and running even as the ink was drying on the tome you now hold in your hands.

And two last sections to recommend. First, "Secret Periodicals." Here, you will find a list of free newspapers and Web sites that will keep you informed on all the up-to-the-minute happenings around town. Second, "Secret Media." Here, you'll get an insider's perspective on where to turn for news, sports, traffic, weather, and entertainment information. I am an admitted media junkie, often spending entire afternoons channel surfing between news broadcasts, even as I hold the newspaper. Because of this, you're in good hands.

Here's the last bit of advice before you dive into this newly revised edition of *Secret Chicago*. Be adventurous. Explore. Get happily lost. When was the last time you did that? Take a summer night and wander to a far-off pocket of the Windy City. Take in the breeze. Listen to the rustle of the trees and the traffic in the distance and the rumble of the elevated train. Hear the laughter of children playing soccer in one of the city's many parks. Smell the aroma of one-dollar tamales being pushed by in a small cart. Marvel at the sunset sinking, sinking ever lower in a melted blur of tropical-flavored sherbet.

As the original mayor Richard M. Daley once said: "This is Chicago, this is America."

SECRET
AFRICAN-AMERICAN

Nearly two million African-Americans call Chicago home, which is nearly 40 percent of the entire metropolitan population. No other place better exhibits the rich history and culture of Chicago's vibrant black community than the **DuSable Museum of African-American History** (740 East 56th Place, 773-947-0600). And the name is fitting as well — Jean-Baptiste Pointe du Sable was the first non-native American to settle the area. In 1779, the Haitian man established a trading post on the Chicago River. Founded in 1961, the DuSable Museum is the oldest museum of African-American history in the United States. Recent exhibits include "State of the Blues: The Living Legacy of the Delta," a photographic testament to the Delta blues by photographer Jeff Dunas. The museum also features a stunning collection of African artifacts, as well as slave documents and the permanent display of the office of the late Harold Washington, the city's popular black mayor from 1983 to 1986.

At the **Woodson Regional Library** (9525 South Halsted Street, 312-747-6900), the Vivian G. Harsh Research Collection of Afro-American History and Literature is the largest collection of its kind in the entire Midwest. Named for the first black librarian in the Chicago Public Library system (Harsh was named the head of the George Cleveland Hall branch in 1932), this voluminous trove of materials contains thousands of documents pertaining to the black experience. And the emphasis, not surprisingly, is on African-American history in Illinois.

The **Afrocentric Bookstore** (333 South State Street, 312-939-1956) is housed on the ground floor of the **Chicago Music Mart** building

(333 South State Street, 312-362-6700) — a grand downtown high-rise primarily dedicated to the sale of fine musical instruments and sheet music. There is also a wonderful CD shop, Crow's Nest (see "Secret CDs"), off the main lobby. Before you even enter the Afrocentric Bookstore, the odds are good you'll hear live classical music fluttering up from the basement courtyard. The Music Mart regularly schedules performances of symphonic orchestras, solo pianists, and even blues and jazz bands. All events are free and open to the public. In the Afrocentric Bookstore, you'll find an amazing selection of black literature (modern and classic), black history, and inspirational materials. There's also an impressive lineup of author signings and readings here. Pick up a copy of *New City* (see "Secret Periodicals") for listings.

One of my absolute favorite places in Chicago is the **South Shore Cultural Center** (7059 South Shore Drive, 312-747-2536). This opulent, turn-of-the century structure is one of the city's best-kept secrets. Often referred to as "the jewel of the South Side," this former country club, built in 1906, sits just a short distance from a beautiful and secluded stretch of beachfront on Lake Michigan (see "Secret Beaches"). Surrounded by a lakefront golf course, the center harkens back to another era. Modeled after a building in Mexico City, the center has terra-cotta-colored columns lining the entrance. Inside, crystal chandeliers twinkle in a scene straight out of F. Scott Fitzgerald's *The Great Gatsby*. In its heyday, the South Shore Cultural Center — with its grand dining room, theater, and solarium — played host to visiting royalty, prominent politicians, and talk-of-the-town celebrities. Among its guests: President William F. Taft, Buffalo Bill Cody, and Edward, Prince of Wales. Tennis champs Bill Tilden and Bobby Riggs played a match here. Will Rogers even entertained at this magnificent structure. Today, the center, sold to the Chicago Park District in 1974, has been rehabbed to its former glory. Its gallery regularly showcases the paintings and photographs of some of Chicago's most talented African-American artists. I like this place so much, I got married here.

SECRET
AL FRESCO

Great outdoor dining should provide a much-needed respite from the hustle and bustle of urban living. When sitting down for an outdoor meal, you don't want wailing car alarms, exhaust fumes, and sirens enveloping you like some sort of chaotic metropolitan tsunami. And you don't want passersby gawking — or, even worse — commenting on your food. True urban al fresco restaurants go beyond plastic lawn furniture set up on a crowded sidewalk. They are an escape from all the metro madness. Searching for an out-of-the-way city oasis? I've got the answer. But remember, I'm talking Chicago here. The outdoor sections of these fine establishments are only open from tulip season to tomato season (that's a mere three to four months).

Forgo the tight front room of **La Creperie** (2845 North Clark Street, 773-528-9050) altogether. Through the narrow hall and beyond the back room is a quaint patio, walled in by adjacent brick buildings. At night, the lights draped above the patio are lit, and an accordion player occasionally wanders from table to table playing "Fly Me to the Moon" or "L'Accordeoniste." Sample a deep glass of merlot and some of the most delectable crepes in all of Chicago.

Corosh (1072 North Milwaukee Avenue, 773-235-0600) provides a splendid al fresco retreat with its overflowing flowerpots, rustic birdhouses, and some of the best modestly priced gourmet Italian in town. The service is exceptional, and they make an amazing cosmopolitan. My old managing editor at *New City* first brought me here, and it's since become a preferred dining spot for the Mrs. and me.

My favorite outdoor dining escape in Chicago is the **Garden Restaurant** (Michigan Avenue, at Adams Street, 312-443-3543). I suppose I'm a little biased. As a young, broke college student, I waited tables here for three summers. Some of my fondest memories are of my days spent working in this incredible environment. Mornings were always the best. The wait staff would arrive at nine in the morning and set up the tables. There were no customers yet, just the laughter and conversation of a crew bonding over these golden, sun-drenched mornings. Once the staff was finished, the museum served us breakfast and then we had half an hour to explore the galleries before they opened to the public. I recall many mornings sitting in a room on a cold stone bench, surrounded by Monet's "Haystack" series.

So about the restaurant . . . enclosed within the Art Institute's courtyard, this epicurean retreat is the museum's very best kept secret. Art Institute patrons often stand next to the cobalt-hued Chagall window, gape down at the museum's interior patio and wonder how to get into the garden, which first opened in the 1930s. The Art Institute, like most museums, is a concentration of marbled halls linked together in one vast, twisting maze. Remember the mythological story of Theseus wandering through the labyrinth to slay the Minotaur? Well, getting to the garden is just about as formidable a task. Here's the secret: at the east entrance of the museum (off Columbus Avenue), hike down the stairs by the old Stock Exchange Room. Turn left at the bottom of the stairs and midway down the hall, on your right side, you will see a pair of white doors. Voila! You've made it.

Once outside, you'll find yourself in a sylvan world. Shaded by towering trees, the expansive fountain, designed by Carl Mills, sits in the middle of the courtyard. It, too, is a work of art. On Tuesdays, the museum stays open until 8 PM, offering up some fabulous jazz sounds within this marbled courtyard. But get there early — 4 PM — if you want a table.

Thyme (464 North Halsted Street, 312-226-4300), with ivy cascading down the walls, offers a contemporary menu full of deceivingly simple concoctions in a beautiful setting. The salads are crisp and uncluttered; the tomato and prosciutto panini is a delight. But watch out — unlike other outdoor dining escapes, Thyme is uncovered and the high sun in the middle of summer can be true torture. Recommendation: sunscreen with maximum SPF.

Moody's Pub (5910 North Broadway Street, 773-275-2696), with its dark wood paneling and crackling fire always burning away in the fireplace, is a great escape on a blustery winter's night (see "Secret Hamburgers"). But with the onset of spring, Moody's opens up its lush two-tiered beer garden. After sitting at one of the patio's 60 tables and devouring a trademark burger with gobs of melted cheese, onions, and mouth-watering tomatoes, you'll never be gripped by another Big Mac attack.

Other outstanding outdoor eateries: **Bar San Miguel** (3313 North Clark Street, 773-871-0896) is casual and low key, and, come evening, a warm glow envelops its patio. The local theater community flocks here, after the curtain has fallen and the lights have dimmed. **Jackson Harbor Grill** (6401 South Coast Guard Drive, 773-288-4442) is the best place to dine near the lake. You can watch sailboats and seagulls in the adjacent South Lakeshore Harbor bob up and down in the lapping waves. Try the banana rum chicken with sweet potato flan — it's marvelous.

SECRET
ANTIQUES

Antiques aren't much of a secret anymore. Countless cable television shows appraise and inspect old collectibles and furniture ad nauseam, making it increasingly difficult to land an antique treasure amidst the must and dust of most shops. But scoring a beautiful addition to your home at a steal of a price is still a possibility. The **Kane County Flea Market** (525 South Randall Road, between routes 38 and 64, St. Charles, 630-377-2252), an hour west of downtown Chicago, is the largest flea market in the entire Midwest. Held on the first Saturday (noon to 5 PM) and Sunday (7 AM to 4 PM) of every month, the fair lures nearly 1,600 dealers — many just farmers selling the tables and fixtures that have sat idle in their barns for decades. The market is set in a group of muddy fields and barns. It's open year round — rain, sleet, blizzard, or heat wave. The best time to go, for the widest selection of wares, is in the summer, when the market opens on Saturday. There's a lot of junk, so be patient. Admission is $5 for adults, free for children under 12. While you're there, visit the nearby town of St. Charles, nestled along the Fox River. You may want to browse through the series of antiques shops downtown. **The Antique Markets I, II, and III**, which have a total of 75 dealers at three locations, carry lots of old jewelry, dishes, furniture, and all-around bric-a-brac. The three stores are all within a two-block radius (11 North Third Street, 630-377-1868; 413 West Main Street, 630-377-5599; 303 West Main Street, 630-377-5798).

But you need not drive outside Chicago to find antiques; several stores are located downtown. I advise you to hop down to the large cluster of stores known as **Antique Sellers Row** (Belmont Avenue,

between Damen Avenue and Western Avenue). You could easily spend an entire afternoon darting in and out of the shops, sorting through piles and piles of old service-station signs, fixer-up furniture, brass doorknobs and knockers, and Art Deco jewelry. Don't miss **Vintage Deluxe** (2127 West Belmont Avenue, 773-529-7008) for a trove of all things 1950s, 1960s, mod, and swinging. This tight one-room store is stuffed with retro treasures. Dig those Hawaiian tikis! Just across the street, **Danger City** (2120 West Belmont Avenue, 773-871-1420) is wall-to-wall kitsch, from circa World War II to the JFK era. Store owners William Smits and Robert Tuttle are friendly and always willing to negotiate. Here, you'll find all sorts of affordable gems, from furniture to lamps to barware to artwork.

Art Deco hounds won't find a better antiques store than **ZigZag** (3419 North Lincoln Avenue, 773-525-1060). Some of the pieces for sale are fabulous — lots of sleek, chrome furniture and Jazz Age light fixtures.

For a mind-blowing antiques experience, visit **Salvage One** (1840 West Hubbard Street, 312-733-0098), the largest salvage company in the country. Here you'll find old furnishings from around the world taken from buildings prior to demolition. There are old bars, bookcases, doors, vanities, chandeliers, church pews, and countless other items. If you are restoring a building of your own, this place is a four-story playground to romp in. This all said . . . Salvage One, at least in this writer's estimation, is way overpriced. It caters to weekend warriors driving SUVs and to restaurant and bar owners with bulging bank accounts. You'll be hard pressed to find a bargain anywhere in this vast warehouse.

When I go antiquing, I trek to the **Broadway Antique Market** (6130 North Broadway Street, 773-868-0285). Again, the prices are a little steep, but the collection is unparalleled. Most everything is in immaculate condition. Owners Danny Alias and Jeff Nelson represent 85 dealers in this 20,000-square-foot space. The market has a nifty assortment of antique watches, a staggering display of '50s dinette tables, Bakelite wares, vintage clothes, hip velvet and paint-by-numbers paintings . . . you name it.

SECRET
ARCHITECTURE

Second City, my ass. Chicago's skyline is the most beautiful display of architecture in the US. Period. And I'm not alone in my opinion. The American Institute of Architects has declared that Chicago has some of the finest architecture in the country. While it may not have the history of Paris or Rome, Chicago proclaims itself the birthplace of modern architecture. From the ashes of the Great Chicago Fire of 1871, the steel-framed skyscraper was born. And with the skyscraper came new building materials and technology: glass and steel and elevators. Chicago didn't earn the nickname "Paris on the Prairie" for nothing. Hyperbole? Hardly. Take a look around, wander the streets, explore the buildings. You will see.

If you only have time for one Windy City tour, the **Chicago Architecture Foundation** (tour centers in the Santa Fe building at 224 South Michigan Avenue, and in the John Hancock Center at 875 North Michigan Avenue, 312-922-3432) is the place to go. Founded in 1966, this not-for-profit organization operates a total of 65 tours in and around the city. There are walking tours of specific buildings, tours by bicycle in the warm months, and very popular tours by

riverboat in summertime. The boats dock on the Chicago River under the shadow and spires of the Tribune Tower. Cruise tickets are $18. The two-hour tour highlights more than 50 architecturally significant buildings along the waterway. It's best to make reservations, however, as the lines for the trips start early. You can call 312-922-TOUR for more info. You won't get a better understanding or appreciation of the city's concrete and steel landscape anywhere else. The foundation also offers tours of Frank Lloyd Wright's Oak Park buildings, local cemeteries, and lesser-known neighborhoods. The CAF has a Web site if you want to learn more: www.architecture.org.

Don't have the time or the wherewithal for an organized tour? Do it yourself. Here's my top-10 list — in no particular order — of the best downtown buildings to explore. These are the structures that, even after years of living in the Windy City, still blow me away. Happy exploring!

Most travel guides will inform you that the **Tribune Tower** (435 North Michigan Avenue) was the winning design in an international competition held by *Chicago Tribune* newspaper publisher Colonel Robert R. McCormick back in 1922. The building was designed by New York architects Raymond Hood and John Howells. Construction was completed in 1925. And that's where most guides stop. Here's a bit more about one of Chicago's most stunning skyscrapers: Hood and Howell snagged a $100,000 prize for their design, beating out 263 other entries from around the world. But my favorite parts of this landmark of Indiana limestone, other than the flamboyant flying buttresses, are the 136 stones embedded on the outside of the building. Walk up and take a look. They are artifacts from some of the most famous structures in the world. The Alamo, the Great Wall of China, the Berlin Wall, the Taj Mahal, Westminster Abbey, the Parthenon — there are stones from all corners of the earth. Many were received as gifts, while some were stealthily gathered by foreign correspondents at the direction of McCormick. Recently, the *Trib* acquired a new geologic addition on indefinite loan from the National Aeronautics and Space Administration — a moon rock. The stone is in a ground-floor window display.

Surely you've seen them. The twin corncobs. When you gaze at **Marina City** (300 North State Street), you immediately know you're in Chicago. Completed in 1967, these buildings, designed by Bertrand Goldberg, were the ultimate swanky Chicago bachelor pads of the early '70s. Here's a crazy tale: in the middle of winter, high up on these 60-story structures, party animals would scale up and down the building on the outside balconies to swap sex partners. As Austin Powers would say: "Yeah, baby!"

All apologies to the taller Sears Tower, but the **John Hancock Center** (875 North Michigan Avenue) is simply more muscular and magnificent. On the observation deck on top of the 1,107-foot skyscraper, you can see the entire city in all directions. And if you are on the ground, stand right at the base and look straight up. The view is dizzying. Around the holidays, the ring of light near the top changes color to reflect the season. There's Halloween orange, Valentine red, St. Patrick green, and other holiday-appropriate colors.

So what if a so-called New Age guru called the diamond shape of the **Stone Container Building** (150 North Michigan Avenue) bad feng shui for the city? (Really, someone said this.) This structure, built in 1983 by A. Epstein and Sons, is one the most striking features of the grand Chicago skyline.

At night, powerful floodlights on the Michigan Avenue bridge illuminate the **Wrigley Building** (400 North Michigan Avenue). This 79-year-old white terra-cotta landmark, the longtime headquarters of the Wrigley chewing gum empire, marks the south end of the Magnificent Mile shopping district. It serves as an example to other property managers of how to care for an aging building. While many old structures in Chicago undergo recurring renovations and major face-lifts, the Wrigley building has never been restored. Instead, like its sibling ballpark — Wrigley Field, where the Cubs play — it has received a regular program of maintenance. Hey, that's a lesson to all you younger structures.

The **Monadnock Building** (53 West Jackson Boulevard) is bold, simple, and elegant. This 1893 masterpiece of masonry reaches 16 floors toward the heavens. With steel interior columns and floor supports, the Monadnock is an impressive construction of red brick. It was the tallest and heaviest load-bearing structure in existence in its time. But in order to support such a monolith, the architects had to construct base walls that are a whopping six feet thick. This was the last skyscraper in Chicago to employ this method of construction before the new era of skyscrapers arrived.

In terms of overall floor space, the **Merchandise Mart** (300 North Wells Street) is the second-largest building in the world. The Mart is so damned big, in fact, that it has its own zip code. In 1931, Chicago retailer Marshall Field commissioned architects Graham, Anderson, Probst & White to build this limestone and terra-cotta colossus, and later sold it to the Kennedy family. The Kennedys, in turn, unloaded the building in 1998 (with other real estate holdings) for a cool $625 million. Today, the building is a wholesale hub of furniture and furnishings maintained by manufacturers for buyers all over the world. In total, there are more than 600 permanent trade showrooms. The 13th floor holds the world's largest display of kitchen and bath wares, and it's open to the public. But the coolest part of the Mart is out front, along the Chicago River. Here you will find the **Merchandise**

Mart Hall of Fame, a display of eight giant bronze busts portraying the bigwigs of industry, from Marshall Field to F.W. Woolworth. What's so interesting about this? They look like giant Pez dispensers. Nighttime is the best time to view the Mart (and the Pez hall of fame), as dramatic lighting floods its façade. And, oh, by the way, the largest building on earth is the Pentagon in Washington, DC.

I'm sentimentally attached to the **Blackstone Hotel** (636 South Michigan Avenue), since I went to undergraduate and graduate school right next door. Built in 1909, the Blackstone is one of Michigan Avenue's most dignified structures. It's also a rare example of the modern French style of Beaux Arts (classical revival) architecture. It earned the nickname "hotel of presidents" after Woodrow Wilson, Theodore and Franklin D. Roosevelt, and John F. Kennedy lodged there. Recently, the hotel was closed and the building, like so many structures in Chicago, went condo.

Not far from the Blackstone, you'll find the **Dearborn Street Station** (47 West Polk Street), a rail station built in 1885 by famed New York architect Cyrus L.W. Eidlitz. This is the city's only surviving 19th-century train station. It stands, with its red brick clock tower, at the southern end of Dearborn Street. The trains stopped running in 1971; the station is now used as a commercial and retail space. Each year in June, the Printers Row Book Fair is centered here (see "Secret Books").

Built in 1885, the **Fine Arts Building** (410 South Michigan Avenue) was originally known as the Studebaker Building (with Studebaker carriages and buggies in the Michigan Avenue showroom windows). It has long been a performing arts center, with studios, craft shops, movie theaters, and concert halls. Architect Frank Lloyd Wright once had an office here. The building's best features are the antique elevators, with their brass fixtures and a live operator who asks "Floor, please?" You can hear violin lessons, or vocalists ranging through scales, echoing down the marble hallways as you pass between floors. And the clickety-clack of the old elevator, in its own way, is music to the ears.

SECRET
BARBECUE

Having lived a few years in Texas, I find there's nothing better than a backwoods barbecue shack off the side of a sleepy two-lane Lone Star state highway. Coming through a screen door that slams shut behind you, you enter a wide-open room with whirling ceiling fans overhead, a jukebox kicking out some country twang, and the overwhelming smell of hickory — a smell that becomes a pleasant, permanent fixture in your clothes and hair. Chicago may not have any true barbecue roadhouses, but we do have some mighty fine BBQ, if you just follow your sniffer. And some of these places even offer up a heapin' helpin' of down-home hospitality. Wipe your feet and put on your bib.

Smoke Daddy Rhythm & Bar-B-Cue (1804 West Division Street, 773-772-6656) serves up true Texarkana-style BBQ. This food is the closest thing in Chicago to that delectable, desolate highway smoke-shack BBQ joint. The 1,900-pound wood-burning pit is the secret. At night, some great live blues bands perform.

And while it's certainly possible to find some good "Q" on the North Side of town, mostly you have to head south to neighborhoods far less familiar to tourists and unadventurous locals.

Leon's Bar-B-Q, with four South Chicago locations (8251 South Cottage Grove Avenue, 773-488-4556; 1640 East 79th Street, 773-731-1454; 1158 West 59th Street, 773-778-7828; 4550 South Archer Avenue, 773-247-4171), is known citywide for some of the best ribs around. After 60 years, owner Leon Finney really knows how to do his BBQ right. The neighborhoods aren't always the safest (as evidenced by the bulletproof glass at the ordering counters), but if food is worth the risk, this is where to go. The Archer location is the perfect pit stop on the way to and from Midway Airport (see "Secret Shortcuts"). For BBQ beef brisket that tastes like it fell straight off the bone, try **Ribs 'n' Bibs** (5300 South Dorchester Avenue, 773-493-0400). The sandwiches are laden with messy sauce and they're cheap. **Lem's Bar-B-Q House** (5914 South State Street, 773-684-5007) is a carryout-only joint in another slightly sketchy part of town, but the ribs are so good it doesn't really matter. Carry some mace if you're worried. These are big, meaty ribs with a choice of a smooth, tangy mild sauce or a Louisiana-style pepper sauce for those who favor some heat.

Sometimes it is absolutely mandatory to venture across city lines. **Hecky's Barbecue** (1902 Green Bay Road, Evanston, 847-492-1182) is one real good reason to head to the suburbs. Better yet, run. The ribs in this little storefront come slathered to taste, from mild to hot. And, oh baby, are they good. Don't forget the baked beans as a side dish!

Care to go a little bit more upscale? The **Blackhawk Lodge** (41 East Superior Street, 312-280-4080) is not a BBQ joint, per se, but it is well known to business travelers as a downtown hotbed for slabs of tender and tasty hickory-smoked ribs. But you'd better save room for dessert. The banana cream pie is out of this world.

S E C R E T
B A S E B A L L

Chicago baseball teams seem to lose a lot more than they win. It's
been 85 years since our South Side franchise, the White Sox, won the
World Series. And the Cubs, the woeful Cubs. Let's not even talk
about them. The last time our lovable North Side losers took baseball's
crown was way, way back, just prior to World War I, in 1908. Just in
case you were wondering, this is the longest streak in professional
sports without a championship. Still, we love our baseball. And there's
plenty of it to be found beyond our two professional franchises.

While I've tried to stay within the asphalt boundaries of Chicago
with this guide, occasionally it's just too tempting to hop in the car
and take a one-hour road trip to some of the great offerings in the
outlying areas. One such secret gem is the **Kane County Cougars**
(Elfstrom Stadium, 34W002 Cherry Lane, Geneva, 630-232-8811), a
Class A minor league farm team for the Florida Marlins. One trek to a
Cougars game proves that baseball is, indeed, the all-American sport.
During night games, as the sun melts on the horizon, freight trains
lumber by just beyond the outfield wall. Domestic beer — unlike the
criminal prices charged at Wrigley Field or Comiskey Park ($4.50
for a 12-ounce cup) — is just $3.25 for a bottomless 22-ounce. The
stadium seats 8,500 fans, with additional space for 4,100 people on
the surrounding lawn. The nicest aspect of a Cougars game is the
distinct flavor of small-town Mayberry provincialism. Here, the players
really are playing for the love of the sport. And a Cougars game is
cheap. Just $8 for box seats, $7 for reserved seats, $6 for the bleachers,
and $5 for lawn seats. But beware, they do tack on an additional $3
service charge.

The **Schaumburg Flyers,** a Class AA equivalent in the fledgling independent Northern League, play in the nearby northwest suburb of Schaumburg. They're at home, on average, 50 games each season (Schaumburg Flyers Stadium, 1999 Springinsguth Road, Schaumburg, 847-891-2255). The stadium holds 7,048 fans. Admission, by baseball standards, is cheap. Reserved club seats are $9; reserved seats are $8; lawn and bleacher seats are $5.

Wanna bat a few balls around yourself? **Sluggers** (3540 North Clark Street, 773-248-0055) sits kitty corner to the friendly confines of Wrigley Field. Avoid the bar downstairs, loaded with keg-fed frat boys and hairsprayed sorority sisters, and head to the second floor to take some cuts at fast, medium, or slow-pitch balls. There are also a few softball cages.

When my sports-mad friends come to town, I always take them to **Sports World** (1027 West Addison Street, 773-472-7701), which is directly across the street from Wrigley Field. Looking for a hat from the 1914 Cubs? Got it. Looking for a hat from the now-defunct Houston 45s? Got it. Minor League ball caps? Got those too, along with hats from the old black leagues; baseball, football, hockey, and basketball jerseys; and posters, plaques, autographed baseballs, and countless other souvenirs. This is a quick fix for a sports junkie.

And finally, for a piece of Cubbie history, a few blocks north of Wrigley Field, stop off at a store that sells actual stadium box seats from the ballpark. The seats were removed a few years ago during renovations. There is a very limited number, and once the seats are gone, they're gone. They come in sets of two and still have the small metal number plates that tell you exactly what seats they were. After years of exposure to the harsh elements, some of them are a tad beat-up, but they clean up well. The neatest parts are the metal armrests, which have been polished to a shiny silver from years of fans rubbing their hands along the tops. If this bit of baseball history interests you, I recommend you call and reserve your set before they're sold out. A pair of box seats goes for $425. Call 773-404-7975 or just drop into the **Stadium Seat Store** (810 West Irving Park Road).

SECRET
BEACHES

Throngs of tourists and leathery-skinned locals flock to **Oak Street Beach** (Oak Street, 1000 North and the lake) each year. The beach, with the Chicago skyline looming almost directly overhead, is impressive, but hardly secret. Another hot spot that deserves mention is **North Avenue Beach** (North Avenue and the lake). Just about every evening in the summer, scores of volleyball players swarm the sand to spike it out at sunset. Bicyclists, inline skaters, joggers, strollers, and dog walkers crowd the bike trail and create a bedlam where the battle cry is the recurring "on your left!" But this book is about the getaways and little treasures and more remote patches frequented by locals in the know. So here's a general rule of thumb to consider: the farther north or south you go from downtown, the more secluded and pristine the beach. The **South Shore Country Club Beach** (71st Street and the lake) has long been a favorite of South Siders fleeing the summer heat. It gets crowded on weekends, but on weekdays, you just may be the only one with your toes in the sand. But, remember, with the average air temperature in July hovering around 81 degrees Fahrenheit, the lake can be quite a cold jolt. During summer, Lake Michigan water temperatures teeter right around 60 degrees. Still, the surf feels delicious on those dog days. Just north

of this stretch is the **63rd Street Beach** (63rd Street and the lake), a favorite with residents. The beach is vast and the old beach house has recently been restored to its original grandeur. On the North Side, **Montrose Beach** (Montrose Avenue and the lake) sprawls out seemingly forever. In the skies overhead, colorful kites flap in the fierce Chicago winds. This beach is quite popular with the doggie population of Chi-town. On summer evenings, the adjacent park comes alive with amateur softball, soccer teams, and families manning charcoal grills that fill the air with olfactory delights — aromas of hot dogs and brats and hamburgers. If you head even farther north, you'll find **Pratt Beach** (Pratt Boulevard and the lake), a true neighborhood retreat. It's a small expanse of sand at the end of a tree-lined street. Don't forget to pick up a sandwich and soda to go at the **White Hen Pantry** (6801 North Sheridan Road, 773-262-0718) along the way. While most convenience store chains charge astronomical prices for viands, White Hen stores prepare some of the cheapest and best deli food in town (see "Secret Delicatessens").

At **Kathy Osterman Beach** (Ardmore Avenue, 5800 North and the lake), the old, elegant, pink Edgewater Beach Apartments serve as a dramatic backdrop to a stretch of slate-smooth sand. Other great fun, sun, and surf retreats include **Foster Beach** (Foster Avenue and the lake), **Lunt Avenue Beach** (Lunt Avenue and the lake) and **Rainbow Park Beach** (76th Street and the lake). These hideaway beaches have sloping soft, sandy bottoms that are perfect for swimming.

S E C R E T

BEER GARDENS

There's nothing better than a frosty pint of ale on a summer afternoon in a quiet outdoor retreat. Beer gardens are a seasonal jubilee, reserved for those months when Chicagoans can get outside and fritter away an afternoon over a bottle of cold suds.

Resi's Bierstube (2034 West Irving Park Road, 773-472-1749) is the exemplary place to start (and end, for that matter) your terrace pub crawl. This cozy, old German restaurant and tavern has a splendid backyard patio and more than 130 brews on tap. After a Cubs game, stop in at **Sheffield's** (3258 North Sheffield Avenue, 773-281-4989). The beer garden is lively and the selection of more than 50 bocks, porters, ales, and pilsners is excellent. Cheers. I give a cautious recommendation to the beer garden at **John Barleycorn Memorial Pub** (658 West Belden Avenue, 773-348-8899). Don't get me wrong, the atmosphere is wonderful, with lots of space and a lighted waterfall. But stay away on weekends if you know what's good for you — this venerable old Chicago pub turns into a meat market. **Cork and Kerry** (10614 South Western Avenue, 773-445-2675) has a fun, roomy decked beer garden with Guinness as the drink of choice. And for a cozy beer garden that's open year round, try the **Village Tap** (2055 West Roscoe Street, 773-883-0817). In fact, the outdoor patio behind this Roscoe Village tavern is even more inviting in the winter months, when snow is falling and the sidewalks are slick with ice. But don't worry, you need not sport thermal long johns and mittens to enjoy a pint of ale — the tavern encloses the patio with a canvas rooftop. And the fireplace helps warm things up, too.

The Red Lion Pub (2446 North Lincoln Avenue, 773-348-2695) is a British-style tavern famous for its fish 'n' chips, hard cider, and ghosts. Yes, that's right, the restaurant is reportedly home to a spirit that clomps around the second-floor bar. A few employees and patrons have sworn they've heard screams emanating from the women's restroom. Others have said they've felt the spine-tingling tap of a phantom on their shoulder. Legend has it that a woman died upstairs at the turn of the last century and her ghost has haunted the pub since. Even if you don't believe, this former bookie joint has a storied history — the building was erected after the Great Chicago Fire of 1871 — and quite possibly the best bar food in the city. And, oh yes, in summer, the rooftop beer garden is a perennial favorite.

S E C R E T
BICYCLING

If you want to get around Chicago by bicycle, rent a bike at any one of the **Bike Chicago** (1-800-915-BIKE) lakefront locations. Take an afternoon and pedal along the city's 18-and-a-half-mile paved lakefront bike path, and I bet you'll come back convinced that Chicago is the most beautiful city for bicycling in the whole country. You can find Bike Chicago at Navy Pier (600 East Grand Avenue), at the Lincoln Park Zoo (2200 North Cannon Drive), and at Buckingham Fountain (Grant Park, at Lake Shore Drive and Congress). Bicycles are $9.75 an hour or $34 a day; locks and safety gear are complimentary. Cool service alert: they deliver bikes to hotels. Another tip: book your bike online at www.bikechicago.com and get 10 percent off. The lakeshore trail begins at **Kathy Osterman Beach** (Ardmore Avenue, 5800 North and the lake) and winds all the way south to the **South Shore Cultural Center** (7059 South Shore Drive, 312-747-2536). And here's a little secret — bike on the south side of the city. The north is loaded (particularly on weekends) with pedestrians, bicyclists, and pets. It can be annoying no matter how beautiful the scenery. The best stretch for solitude is from Buckingham Fountain south.

While Chicago is unquestionably a gorgeous setting for a bike ride, it isn't particularly bike-friendly. Don't even attempt to ride along the Magnificent Mile (or anywhere in the Loop, for that matter) unless you are a serious cyclist. Professional bike messengers have long battled to get cab drivers to stay off the designated bike lanes. The **Chicagoland Bicycle Federation** (650 South Clark Street, 312-427-3325) is a nonprofit advocacy group that has tried to improve the world bicyclists ride in. Because of this cool group, there are more bike racks and bike lanes in Chicago than ever before. The city is car dominated, but the CBF works hard to integrate bikes into the mix. Also, it publishes a very detailed bicycling map of Chicago for $6.95. You can pick up a free, although less detailed, map from the **Chicago Department of Transportation** (30 North LaSalle Street, Suite 400, 312-744-4686). Just ask for the Chicagoland Bicycle Map.

Countless bicycle events in the city are held throughout the summertime. One that really stands out is the **L.A.T.E. Ride** (773-918-RIDE). It's sponsored by **Friends of the Parks** (55 East Washington Street, Suite 1911, 312-922-3307), a nonprofit park and lakefront advocacy group. This 25-mile ride, held each July, attracts 10,000 bicyclists. They gather before midnight at Buckingham Fountain in Grant Park on Saturday night and pedal until dawn — hence the acronym L.A.T.E. (Long After Twilight Ends). What makes this so much fun is the sheer number of bicyclists. But the going is slow, which is great for neophytes and not so great for hardcore cyclists. The ride takes you downtown past skyscrapers, through Greek Town and Lincoln Park, and eventually back along the city's moonlit lakefront. Along the way you stop for snacks at rest stops, and by sunrise, when you've reached the very end, there's a post-ride breakfast waiting at Buckingham Fountain.

The Chicago Park District manages more than 20 bike paths in the city. And while the lakefront route is the most popular, the **North Branch Bicycle Trail** (begins at Caldwell Avenue and Devon Avenue) is a treasured ride among bicycle purists. Ride along this picturesque path and you'll follow the bends and curves of the north branch of the Chicago River. If you're hardcore, you can pedal all the way up to the north suburb of Highland Park. It's a 20-mile trek, but if you make it to the finish line, you will be in the beautiful Chicago Botanic Garden (see "Secret Gardens").

<h2 style="text-align:center">SECRET
BIRD-WATCHING</h2>

Aficionados call it "birding." And Chicago is a grand place to do it. Bird-watching. You know, creeping through a thicket of shrubbery with a pair of high-powered field binoculars and eyeing a black-throated blue warbler. More than 300 species of birds fly through Chicago and Cook County every year. There is also an occasional appearance by an oddball stray, known as a "vagrant." On average, birders spot 70 or 80 different species of vagrants a year in the Chicagoland area. If you're lucky and keep a watchful eye, you just might spot a ruff — a European sandpiper that has made a mysterious appearance in Chicago. So why do birds not indigenous to the area pop up every so often? Most experts believe that storms simply throw them off course. Others maintain that it has to do with availability of food. Whatever the cause may be, Chicago is a bird-lover's paradise.

If you really want to get a crash course on the Chi-town winged population, you should start with a visit or phone call to the **Chicago Audubon Society** (5801 North Pulaski Road, 773-539-6793). It conducts field trips and weekly bird walks through **Jackson Park** (6401 South Stony Island Avenue, 312-747-6187). At the **Paul H. Douglas Sanctuary**, AKA the Wooded Island, you will find one of the city's best spots for birding. The land was initially landscaped as a bird sanctuary in 1893 for the World's Columbian Exposition. Nearly 300 species have been spotted often here.

The **Sanctuary** in Lincoln Park, just south of Addison Avenue near the lakeshore, is a very dense, fenced-off, wooded area. While it isn't open to the public, bird-watching is good along the periphery. Waterfowl seem to favor the wetlands of the **North Village Nature Center** (5801 North Pulaski Road, 312-744-5472), where the Chicago Audubon Society, not surprisingly, has its office and conducts more guided tours. Along with a host of herons, egrets, and kingfishers, you'll find a grove of reeds and colorful wildflowers. Most birding experts, however, will direct you to **Montrose Harbor** (4400 North Montrose Avenue at Lake Michigan, 312-747-7226), to a spot called "the Magic Hedge." During the 1960s, this area was a US missile site, with trees lining the fence that surrounded the complex. Today, the weapons are gone, but the bank of trees is still here, providing a perfect spot for nesting. You can get to this area by heading east on Montrose Avenue toward the lake and harbor. Turn right at the fish-bait shop after the harbor and go another 100 feet or so. You'll

discover a wild growth of shrubs, grasses, and small trees. Recently, the Chicago Park District has let the area around the hedge grow wild, making the entire area ideal for migrant birds. Among some of the feathered friends you might spy: common loons, horned grebes, merlins, and snow buntings.

If you're out and about in the 'burbs, don't miss the **Morton Arboretum** (4100 Route 53, 630-968-0074), with 1,500 acres of woodlands, wetlands, and prairie grass. This bucolic retreat was established by Morton Salt Company founder Joy Morton in 1922. It's an ideal place to picnic and bird-watch.

The strangest birding experience in all of Chicago can be found at 53rd Street and the lakefront in the Hyde Park neighborhood. Here you will discover a swarm of bright green monk parakeets living in the wild. These noisy critters hail from southern Latin America, mostly Argentina and Brazil. But they have adapted nicely to the Windy City. According to some University of Chicago research, parakeets were first spotted in Hyde Park in 1973. Birders theorize that a pair of escaped pets pulled a Noah's Ark maneuver to repopulate the species. Some Chicagoans, annoyed by the noise and droppings, have tried to rid the city of these pests, but to no avail. Supposedly, the late mayor, Harold Washington, even had them nesting outside his Hyde Park apartment window.

SECRET
BLUES

Chicago is the electric blues capital of planet Earth. Accordingly, there are almost too many venues to choose from. The best fit the old stereotypes. Good blues bars are crowded, smoky clubs on the shady side of town, with crackling window neon awash on rain-slicked streets and the constant din of beer bottles clanking behind the bar. On a small stage, weathered bands belt out songs of the aching heart, the aching soul, the aching spirit. All of this is juiced up and jammed out from time-tested, faithful electric guitars and tattered amplifiers. This is Chicago blues.

It started back in the 1930s, when blues players migrated north from the Mississippi Delta and Louisiana among the thousands of field workers who were looking for better-paying jobs in Chicago's burgeoning industries. These musicians — used to playing on moonlit, creaky front porches at the end of a long, hot day — found themselves in the midst of a cold brick and steel city. It didn't take long before these bluesmen were influenced by the wave of big-band jazz popular in Chicago. The Delta blues had been infected with urban sophistication. And then came the electric guitar.

Today, in Chicago, the blues is more popular than ever before. There are blues clubs scattered all over town. But here are a few of the real McCoys. **Buddy Guy's Legends** (754 South Wabash Avenue, 312-427-0333) is the place to be. While the surrounding South Loop neighborhood is being cleaned up fast, there's still enough tarnish to lend an authentic vibe to the club. Having a few ratty liquor stores down the block helps, as do the screeching wheels of the Orange Line El train overhead. Buddy Guy, as you probably know, is a deity in blues circles. He's played with them all: Muddy Waters, John Lee Hooker, and Howlin' Wolf. He's also snagged himself a few Grammy Awards along the way. While this place is a bit of a Hard Rock Café for blues enthusiasts (i.e., it caters heavily to tourists), with all of the plaques and pictures and guitars hanging about the room, it draws the very best in national and local blues artists. But arrive late — it doesn't get hoppin' until after 11 PM.

For a real dose of authentic Chicago blues, the **Checkerboard Lounge** (423 East 43rd Street, 773-624-3240) looks, feels, and sounds the way a blues joint should — rough and ragged. The legendary tale of the Rolling Stones showing up for an impromptu jam session is true, and you can see why Mick and the boys chose this South Side shrine. It is the archetypal blues venue. It's intimate, smoky, and threadbare, and a hell of a lot cheaper than the humdrum downtown joints. The club first opened in 1972, fostering the careers of Junior Wells and Buddy Guy among many others. Today, if you can capture Chicago blues journeyman John Primer, a semi-regular performer at the club, you'll get the real deal.

As long as we're talking about the South Side of Chicago, where Chicago blues first sprouted, the **Celebrity Lounge** (4830 South Cottage Grove Avenue, 773-548-4812) is an oft-overlooked location you blues fanatics should frequent. This one-story club occupies a barren area of empty lots and tired buildings, but the scene inside is anything but sleepy. The smoky front room is furnished with a juke-box loaded with great blues gems. The back room is where to find the live music. Saturday nights are a good time to pay a visit, as the house band, Fred Johnson and the Checkmates (fronted by the club's owner, Fred Johnson), takes to the stage, getting the place all hot and sweaty in a hurry and a fury. And best of all, there's no cover charge. On other nights, you may catch surprise blues artists like B.B. King's

impressive daughter, Shirley King, ripping the roof off the joint. The
Celebrity lacks the polish of the more popular blues clubs, and that's
why it wails.

Waxing upscale, **Blue Chicago** (736 North Clark Street and 536
North Clark Street, 312-661-0100) is a fabulous two-for deal. With a
duo of locations almost within spitting distance of each other, one
cover gets you into both venues. If you don't like one, you can always
head to the other. But because this is in the middle of the glitzy
River North district, it is more for tourists than purists. Still, the clubs
book top-name acts. But in my opinion, when a blues club opens its
own merchandise store (734 North Clark Street), the owners don't
have the blues no mo', they got the greens.

Other places worth checking out include **Kingston Mines** (2548
North Halsted Street, 773-477-4646) — you'll find big-name artists
and big-time yuppie crowds in this popular North Side establishment.
And then there's **B.L.U.E.S.** (2519 North Halsted Street, 773-528-
1012). Otis Rush, Sun Seals — need I say more? Yes. More of that
aforementioned young upwardly mobile crowd that valet-parked to
get into the place. Listen to that guitar solo! No wait, that's my cell
phone ringing!

But the big boy on the Chicago blues scene is the **Chicago Blues Fest**
(Grant Park, 312-744-3315), a two-day blowout held on the second
weekend of June. This thing is no secret — the 2001 fest pulled in
660,000 people. But the music is free. The drinks, t-shirts, corn-dogs,
and jambalaya are not. In fact, the prices are enough to give anyone
the blues. Eat and drink beforehand, be merry at the fest.

One more tip: if you are in Chicago on Monday nights, tune in to
radio station **93.1 WXRT** for "Blues Breakers," a phenomenal program
of music and interviews hosted by XRT DJ/bluesologist Tom Marker.

atthew   HEGEWI   R0446080709   12/11/2020

SECRET
BOCCE BALL

Bocce ball dates back a long, long way. Some argue that ancient hieroglyphics portray Egyptians tossing wooden balls on flat courts. One story even finds Sir Francis Drake refusing to interrupt his game to address a threatening military advance. "First we finish the game, then we deal with the advance!" it is believed he proclaimed. Today, in Chicago, particularly in the Italian-American community, bocce is alive and well. And there's no better place to play than in a little sliver of a park on the city's quiet Northwest Side. Evenings in **Hiawatha Park** (8029 West Forest Preserve Avenue, 312-746-5559), an older Italian neighborhood, have a rhythm all their own. During the summer, the setting sun blankets the area in a warm ember-glow. Each night, a crowd of bocce ball regulars arrives from the surrounding neighborhood, like cowboys approaching a gunfight. Even greater in numbers are the spectators, who gather here from roughly 7 PM to 10 PM. Some nights, as competition grows fierce, the games go much later. There are two courts — called "campos" — in Hiawatha Park, each one a 76-by-10-foot clay roadway, with plywood borders painted a deep moss green. This is where the action takes place. Newcomers are always welcome and always invited in on the game. Some of the diehards can even be spotted in this little park on mild winter nights.

In the far southwest corner of the city, in the blue-collar Hegewisch neighborhood, bocce players gather at **Bogey's** (2725 East 130th Street, 773-646-2335), a tavern with a beer garden that has a three-lane court open to the public. A women's league plays on Tuesday evenings and disabled kids play on Wednesdays.

Another bocce hot spot is **McGuane Park** (2901 South Poplar Avenue, 312-747-6497). Here, you'll find a robust crowd playing on three courts and maybe even wagering on a game or two. Don't tell.

S E C R E T
BOOKS
❀

While New York gets props for being America's literary Mecca, Chicago has quite a bookish history as well. Writer H.L. Mencken once called Chicago "the literary capital of the world." Some writers who have called the Windy City home include Ernest Hemingway, Richard Wright, Nelson Algren, Gwendolyn Brooks, Theodore Dreiser, Saul Bellow, Ray Bradbury, Edgar Rice Burroughs, and Carl Sandburg. The list goes on and on and on. Sure, it's a predominantly white male group, but the contemporary Chicago literary scene is loaded with women writers making up for lost time. V.I. Warshawski creator Sara Peretsky calls Chicago home, as does author Rosellen Brown, who recently had a short story named to the *Best Short Stories of the Century* collection by John Updike. Brown also teaches creative writing at the School of the Art Institute. Reflecting this rich tradition of literature, Chicago has a score of great bookshops and literary events.

The best bookstores in town, again, aren't the chain stores, even if they do have lower prices and more books. You know what? Atmosphere still counts. **Barbara's Bookstore,** with four downtown stores and one suburban location (233 South Wacker Drive, 312-466-0223; 1350 North Wells Street, 312-642-5044; 700 East Grand Avenue, 312-222-0890; 2 North Riverside Plaza, 312-258-8007; 1100 Lake Street, Oak

Park, 708-848-9140), is a great place to find small and independent press books. The staff is highly knowledgeable and, at the Wells Street location, visiting authors read from their work in the children's section. **Seminary Co-Op Bookstore** (5757 South University Avenue, 773-752-4381) may well be the world's largest academic bookstore, with more than 100,000 titles. This maze-like bookstore, which winds below an actual seminary, is a favorite haunt of University of Chicago students. And it's no wonder, since they own a good chunk of it. This bookseller has, for years, offered discounts to students as long as they purchase 10 $3 shares of stocks in the store. Just think, a measly 30 bucks and you can own a bookstore! At last count, there were 44,000 owners. For gay and lesbian material, as well as a great selection of general books, stop at **Unabridged Bookstore** (3251 North Broadway Street, 773-883-9119). The staff, versed on all sorts of prose, poetry, and nonfiction, is just one example of the ways small indie stores can trump the chains.

If you're looking for scholarly titles or deeply discounted remaindered books, you won't do any better than at **Powell's** (2850 North Lincoln Avenue, 773-248-1444; 828 South Wabash Avenue, 312-341-0748; 1501 East 57th Street, 773-955-7780). Each of the three locations carries an average of 200,000 titles. You'll also find tons of used, rare, and out-of-print books, hard-to-find imports, and the store's own line of Oxford University Press reprints.

For some of the best author programming in the city, try **57th Street Bookstore** (1301 East 57th Street, 773-684-1300). This shop, along with Powell's and Seminary Co-op, is yet one more reason why the Hyde Park neighborhood is truly a reader's paradise.

If you're lucky enough to be in Chicago on the first weekend of June, wander down to the **Printers Row Book Fair**, a true bookworm's delight. Bounded by Congress Parkway on the north, Polk Street on the south, Dearborn Street on the east, and Clark Street on the west, the fair is the largest of its kind in the entire Midwest. The two-day event includes hundreds of booksellers of new and used books, antiquarian dealers, and a mélange of literary programming that deftly reflects the diverse cultural fabric of Chicago. With great author seminars, musical guests, and wonderful reading events for children, it's no wonder 70,000 people show up annually to this festival.

SECRET
BOOZE

❧

Every city has its designated cheap beer. Chicago's official swill is Old Style. Chicagoans love this Wisconsin brew, with its thin, somewhat sweet, syrupy aftertaste. It's a mystery to me — I hate the shit. So where are the best places to pick up a bottle of booze, whatever your libation inclination? Here are my recommendations.

Sam's Liquors (1720 North Marcey Street, 312-664-4394) is definitely the biggest, and quite possibly the best, store to start your bender. Best known for its wine selection — 300,000 bottles in all — this warehouse is a one-stop shop that even has a basketball hoop for shoppers to take a few jump shots. Employees at this 34,000-square-foot store also boast that they sell more champagne annually than any other store in the United States.

At **Chalet Wine & Cheese Shop** (405 West Armitage Avenue, 773-266-7155; 1531 East 53rd Street, 773-324-5000; 40 East Delaware Place, 312-787-8555), you'll find a huge stock of wine and spirits and cheese, marvelous cheese.

I've been downtown on many a wintry night, on my way to a friend's high-rise party, and come to the "oh-damn-I-didn't-bring-anything" realization. Enter **Binny's Beverage Depot** (213 West Grand Avenue, 312-332-0012). This well-stocked River North superstore is an oasis of alcohol. What you won't find are fancy crackers, Brie cheese, or hickory-smoked sausage. What you will find is booze, lots of booze. If you are a fan of Bordeaux wine or single-malt scotch, you've arrived. When you're in the heart of the city, it's not easy stumbling onto a cavernous emporium that carries everything from a vintage Cabernet Sauvignon to an Olde English 40-ouncer. Thank you, Binny's.

SECRET
BOWLING

I love the neighborhood around Midway Airport. It just sweats Chicago style and character. Within earshot of the planes taking off and landing is the city's coolest and, more importantly, least-known bowling Mecca. **Miami Bowl** (5023 South Archer Avenue, 773-585-8787) has 80 lanes in all, along with a dozen or so pool tables, an arcade, a snack shop, and a lounge. Best of all, Miami Bowl is open 24 hours a day, seven days a week, all year long. Even Christmas. It's a little out of the way, but bowling doesn't get better than a 24-hour lane with computerized scoring and air conditioning. It's a great place to go when you can't think of anything else to do.

All the way across town, on the North Side, is **Southport Lanes & Billiards** (3325 North Southport Avenue, 773-472-1601), a longtime fixture in the Lakeview neighborhood. For more than 77 years this raucous tavern (and former speakeasy and brothel) has been known for its four hand-set bowling lanes. Only 11 bowling alleys in North America certified by the American Bowling Congress still use pin-boys (and girls). This is one. Tips are kindly appreciated, so on the last frame, roll a bill into one of the ball's holes for the pin-people. For billiards fans, Southport Lanes has a side room with pool tables.

Waveland Bowl (3700 North Western Avenue, 773-472-5900) is another 24-hour alley, but it gets packed with rowdy teenagers, especially on weekends, and can be a tad obnoxious. But for the rowdiest time, toss back a couple of beers and bowl to loud rock music and a dizzying light show at the **Diversey Rock-n-Bowl** (2211 West Diversey Avenue, 773-227-5800).

SECRET

BOYSTOWN

The area known as Boystown is the nucleus of Chicago's gay community. The city has many unofficial neighborhoods, like Wrigleyville, the Gold Coast, Bronzeville, and Roscoe Village; these are nicknames, really. Depending on whom you ask, the parameters of these areas may vary slightly. The boundary lines of Boystown, too, are ambiguous. Most people will tell you that it starts on the north at Grace Street and Broadway Street and heads south to Diversey Avenue. On the east side, it extends from Grace Street down Halsted Street to Belmont Avenue. The symbolic focal point of this community is, without question, the annual **Chicago Gay and Lesbian Pride Parade** (773-384-8243), a bombastic festival that attracts 200,000 people.

Held every year at the end of June, the parade features more than 250 floats, cars, and groups along Halsted Street and Belmont Avenue. The parade is a crazy, fun event, with gay militia troops wearing grass skirts, carrying pink rifles, and marching in unison. Local celebrities show up to lend their support to the community. There's live music, outlandish costumes, and unbridled partying. But it's also an important event — a time to discover where the local and state politicians stand on gay rights and a time for gays and lesbians to stand up and proudly proclaim their sexual orientation.

But Boystown isn't just a one-weekend-a-year neighborhood. Here are just a few of the more popular establishments that keep the party going 365 days. **Spin** (800 West Belmont Avenue, 773-327-7711) is a dark, bustling bar blasting out the dance tunes. It has drag shows and video DJs. Remember them? Just a few blocks outside Boystown is **Berlin** (954 West Belmont Avenue, 773-348-4975), a fixture of Chicago's gay scene. It's a wild place with disco nights, drag contests, and a bevy of buff male dancers. Wednesday is ladies' night — that is, an evening for our lesbian sisters. On Wednesday nights at **GirlBar** (2625 North Halsted Street, 773-871-4210), the opposite is the case. It's guys' night! The rest of the week this is an all-girls club. Looking for leather? Try **Manhole** (3458 North Halsted Street, 773-975-9244). This bar is a bit raw — often airing gay porn on corner TVs and requiring boys and girls to remove their shirts in the back room. Leather jackets are okay. No vinyl shit please. **Roscoe's** (3354 North Halsted Street, 773-281-3355) is a mega-popular neighborhood-style bar for the boys. **Sidetrack** (3349 North Halsted Street, 773-477-9189) is a huge video bar that plays everything from old school disco to the latest pop dance tunes. It also hosts the annual "Night of a Thousand Drag Queens" contest. It may not be a thousand, but it's a lot. Like Roscoe's, this place is super popular with guppies.

Looking for something a little seedier, a little nastier? **Lucky Horse-shoe Lounge** (3169 North Halsted Street, 773-404-3169) is a gay club with nightly strip shows starting at 8 PM.

For a complete list of local businesses in Boystown and beyond serving Chicago's lesbian, gay, and bisexual community, look for the **Alternative Phonebook** (773-472-6319; www.apb-chicago.com). This is a free gay yellow pages distributed throughout the Windy City at many record stores, convenience stores, bookshops, and apparel outlets.

SECRET
BREAKFAST

Everything about **Lou Mitchell's** restaurant, opened in 1923 (565 West Jackson Boulevard, 312-939-3111), is classic — starting with the crackling orange neon sign hanging over the entrance. The stainless steel coffee urn is so old, it's no longer even manufactured. But, worry not, like the neon out front, the urn is maintained with TLC by the management of Mitchell's. And, proving that they don't make 'em like they used to, the coffee is perfect and rich. Even the cooks at Lou Mitchell's are of a different era — one of them has been working over the griddle for 42 years. And all of this old-fashioned quality shows in the food. The pancakes and omelettes are huge and fluffy; entrées come with a large wedge of Greek toast and a side of delicious orange marmalade. The portions are too big and the place can get too loud, but that's why it's so damned wonderful.

The Bagel Restaurant and Deli (3107 North Broadway Street, 773-477-0300) is another great breakfast stop-off. It serves mouth-watering Jewish-American fare, which includes an assortment of blintzes, potato pancakes, and omelettes, and bottomless bowls of matzo ball soup. And, of course, it offers about a dozen varieties of bagels. The New York deli–style pickles served with every meal are a nice touch, too.

For breakfast with a decidedly Southern spin, try **Wishbone** (1001 West Washington Boulevard, 312-850-2663). Its atmosphere is open and urban, with all the exposed duct work and colorful artwork on the walls. House specialties include shrimp and grits, blackened catfish, salmon cakes, corn cakes, and the popular red eggs, an Alka-Seltzer-in-waiting-entrée of two eggs served on corn tortillas with black beans, ancho chile sauce, and cheese.

Bongo Room (1470 North Milwaukee Avenue, 773-489-0690) is another artsy little enclave with an eclectic menu that changes regularly. You'll find savory breakfasts that include everything from brown sugar pecan pancakes to superb eggs benedict with a made-to-perfection hollandaise sauce. And the people-watching in this little storefront is hilarious. Bongo Room is in the heart of the trendy Wicker Park neighborhood, where starving artists are fighting a losing battle to fend off developers and yuppies.

One of my favorite greasy breakfast joints is called, simply enough, the **Coffee Shop** (600 North Lasalle Drive, 312-943-6000). You won't find it in other travel guides. It's too small, too secret. As the aging cook and wait staff will tell you, the restaurant hasn't changed an iota since it opened in 1960. There's nothing trendy about this place. They just serve good traditional breakfasts of eggs and hash browns and pots and pots of hot black coffee.

SECRET

CAMPING

Sick and tired of the city? It happens. Lots of Chicagoans flee on weekends to Wisconsin and Michigan for a chance to camp out under the stars. So where does a city person stock up on camping gear? **Erehwon Mountain Outfitter** (1800 North Clybourn Avenue, 312-337-6400) is rife with mountain gear. In this outdoorsy wonderland, you'll find tents made of durable space-age materials, miniature cooking stoves, gargantuan backpacks, hiking boots, and loads of super-cozy down sleeping bags. Erehwon also stocks lanterns, snow-shoes, rain gear, and water purifiers — not to mention that icky freeze-dried food that astronauts supposedly ate. And one more thing: the scattered parking lots around this 30-year-old Chicago store will prep you for any would-be mishaps in the woods. You think a grizzly bear is bad? Think again. Sport utility vehicles blaring horns. People on cell phones giving each other the finger. Fender benders. Cops writing tickets. This is a hostility voyeur's dream come true. Better buy that Swiss army knife; you may need it.

SECRET

CDs

No surprise, but the chain stores have the largest music selection to be found in Chicagoland. **Tower Records/Videos/Books** (2301 North Clark Street, 773-477-5994; 214 South Wabash Avenue, 312-

987-9044) has a stellar stock of classical, jazz, pop, country, and movie soundtracks. It also has a prodigious selection of world music, from Parisian café accordion tunes to the Aboriginal music of the Australian outback. The **Virgin Megastore** (540 North Michigan Avenue, 312-645-9300) gets grades for location, location, location. Conveniently located on the Magnificent Mile, this massive trove of popular music stocks three floors' worth of CDs. Whoever the chief music buyers are for **Hear Music** (932 North Rush Street, 312-951-0242), they're friggin' geniuses. This national chain of five shops was purchased by Starbucks in 1999, but don't hold that against it. The selection at Hear Music is small but always incredibly interesting. The premise at Hear is not about the Top 40. It's about world music, indie rock, roots country, traditional blues, and all the hip stuff usually way off the radar of most mainstream music critics and listeners. As the store's name implies, you can listen to anything before purchasing it.

If you suffer from corporophobia, and you just can't handle chain stores with chain employees, you should definitely check out **Crow's Nest** (333 South State Street, 312-341-9196). This place has the inventory of the big guys, but the attitude and expertise of the little guys. It also has a cyclopedic library of import titles.

Now on to the one-shot, ma and pa, first-and-last little shops where you're bound to unearth that musical treasure. For indie-label rock rarities, pay a call on **Evil Clown** (3416 North Halsted Street, 773-472-4761). For the best selection and prices on used CDs, head to **Dr. Wax** (5225 South Harper Avenue, 773-493-8696; 2523 North Clark Street, 773-784-3333; 1203 North State Street, 312-255-0123). This trio of stores also buys just about any used CD you may have collecting dust. Another cool used CD shop that has great in-store appearances by alternative rock bands is **Reckless Records,** with two locations (3157 North Broadway Street, 773-404-5080; 2055 West North

Avenue, 773-235-3727). Reckless also stocks an abundance of old vinyl. If you're looking for house music, rap, or electronica, try **Hot Jams** (5012 South Pulaski Road, 773-581-5267). Half of the entire store is dedicated to house music.

In Europe, hard rock and heavy metal are as popular as they've ever been. And for eight years, **Impulse Music** (344 East Irving Park Road, Roselle, 630-529-3070) has been a gold mine of imported and very rare metal. If you can't make the 45-minute drive from the city, the store does a lot of mail order at www.impulsemusic.com. My recommendation: the Wildhearts, a snotty Brit-pop-punk outfit mostly unavailable on US soil. It's Cheap Trick meets the Sex Pistols mugged by old KISS. If you can't find the Wildhearts, try their front man's newest band, Silver Ginger 5. It's the best band you're not listening to. Catchy. Melodic. Rocking.

SECRET
CHICAGO FIRE

Everybody's heard of Mrs. O'Leary's cow. On October 8, 1871, around 9 PM, the bovine (named Daisy, Madeline, or Gwendolyn in various incarnations of the tale) kicked over a lantern in the family barn, thus igniting the Great Chicago Fire. Some claimed that Mrs. O'Leary privately confessed that she was in the barn at the time the blaze began. Officially, Kate O'Leary contended that she was in bed early that night and not out milking the cows. An official inquiry supported her claim, finding no evidence that the cow was a pyromaniac or that O'Leary was somehow negligent.

In total, the Great Chicago Fire destroyed more than 18,000 buildings, leveled 100,000 homes, torched 2,000 acres, including 28 miles
of streets and 120 miles of sidewalks, and killed nearly 300 people.
As for the culprit behind the blaze: not found. Most historians have
exonerated Mrs. O'Leary and her cow. Theories range from kids
smoking a cigarette near the barn to meteor fragments striking the
area. While the meteor theory may seem farfetched, experts point to
a similar conflagration in Pestigo, Wisconsin, that raged on the same
night as the Chicago blaze. The Wisconsin fire was the most devastat-
ing forest fire in US history; 1,300 people were killed and a million
acres were lost. On the same night. Coincidence? Hmmm.

Today, most travel guides gloss over the fire as an opportunity for the
smoldering city to reinvent itself. Chicago was, indeed, in cinders and
it gave urban planners a second chance to rethink the layout. Certainly,
the Chicago we know today is a direct result of rebuilding after the
fire. But what many guides ignore is the devastation and the loss. A
few reminders of this great fire still exist today.

The most famous survivor of the fire is the **Water Tower** (806 North
Michigan Avenue, 312-467-7114), one of the city's most beloved and
enduring symbols. Constructed in 1869, this sandcastle-like structure
was built around a 138-foot water pipe. Today, it's non-operational
but stands right in the heart of the Magnificent Mile, a symbol of
the city's perseverance. But, contrary to what most tourists are told,
the Water Tower wasn't the only survivor of the big blaze. **Old St.
Patrick Church** (140 South Des Plaines Street, 312-648-1021) was
built in 1856 and survived the fire. It is the oldest church in Chicago.
Another house of worship that was spared (miraculously, some believe)
by the flames was **Holy Family Church** (1080 West Roosevelt Road,
312-738-4080). As the legend goes, when the fire was spreading,
Father Damen vowed that if his house was kept safe, he would keep

seven lights burning in the church forever. To this day, the lights still burn.

There's a beautiful stained-glass image of the fire along the east wall of the **Chicago Temple First Methodist Church** (77 West Washington Street, 312-236-4548). All the windows on this wall capture the history of the temple in Chicago. The **Chicago Fire Academy** (558 West De Koven Street, 312-747-7238) trains new firefighters every year. It also stands on the exact spot where the O'Leary home and barn once stood. There is a beautiful gold statue by sculptor Egon Weiner outside the facility that commemorates the tragedy.

If you want to learn more about the Great Chicago Fire of 1871, the **Chicago Historical Society** has a very informative Web site at www.chicagohs.org/fire.

One last note: on October 7, 1997, the Chicago City Council approved a resolution that absolved Mrs. O'Leary's cow of all blame for the Great Chicago Fire.

SECRET
CHINESE

No question, Chicago's Chinatown doesn't compare to New York's or San Francisco's. The main strip is only a few blocks long; the square is eerily empty except during special events like the Lunar New Year. But still, some top-notch restaurants exist in this little pocket of town. **Hong Min** (221 West Cermak Road, 312-842-5026) is everything you would ever want in a Chinese eatery. It's a dive with amazing food. This two-room, humble establishment serves some of the best wonton noodle soup to be found — anywhere. The

menu is an encyclopedia of Chinese cuisine. Even Charlie Trotter, Chicago's première chef for people with more money than God, is a fan. And one more super feature about Hong Min: it stays open until 2 AM on weekdays and 3 AM on Fridays and Saturdays. Just a few blocks away, at **Moon Palace** (216 West Cermak Road, 312-225-8800), the specialty is hot and sour soup and Szechwan eggplant with garlic sauce. It's more chic than its neighbors. With two Chinatown locations, **Three Happiness** (209 West Cermak Road, 312-842-1964; 2130 South Wentworth Avenue, 312-791-1229) is the place for dim sum lunch. On weekends at the Wentworth location, the locals wait in line for a place in the massive dining room upstairs. Avoid the first floor — it's not nearly as fun and lively. Upstairs, huge tables with a lazy Susan in the center are perfect for a large family or group of friends. Servers swing around the tables with carts loaded up with all sorts of mouth-watering dumplings, steamed buns, glutinous desserts, and other à la carte goodies. A word of caution: don't sit toward the back of the dining room, as the carts are slower to come by and when they do stop at your table, the pickings are slim.

If you don't want to hoof it to Chinatown, even though it's centrally located and the CTA Red Line (see "Secret El") stops at its entrance (Cermak/Chinatown stop), there are a few Chinese restaurants in other parts of the city worth noting. For 80 years, **Orange Garden** (1942 Irving Park Road, 773-525-7479) has served reliably good Cantonese-style Chinese fare. And the real allure of this place: the decor has changed little in over three quarters of a century. From the silver Art Deco sign above the front door to the black and white checked floors to the Chinese murals on the walls, it's clear that time stopped somewhere in the early 1920s. **Mars** (3124 North Broadway Street, 773-404-1600) offers up great seafood dishes. Try the house specialty, Kung Pao shrimp, for a spicy kick in the ass.

SECRET

CHOCOLATE

In March 1999, **Marshall Field's** (111 North State Street, 312-781-1000), the well-loved, longtime Windy City department store, pissed off all of Chicago. And they really pissed off Mayor Richard M. Daley, which, as any Chicagoan worth his weight in Polish sausage will tell you, is a bad move. For 70 years, on the 13th floor of the Field's flagship store on State Street, a seven-day-a-week, 22-hour-a-day candy kitchen manufactured some of the city's most beloved sweets — **Frango Mints**. For many locals and tourists, a shopping spree at Field's simply was not complete without buying a box of the delectable chocolate-covered mints. But then Dayton Hudson Corporation, the parent company of Field's, abruptly announced it was closing up shop and outsourcing the confection to a chocolatier in Pennsylvania. Pennsylvania, for God's sake! Chicago has definitely been knocked around recently. First da Coach got canned — Mike Ditka was given his walking papers by the Bears. Then the Sears Tower, the longtime tallest-building-champion-of-the-world, was eclipsed by some monstrosity in Malaysia. And as if that wasn't bad enough, Michael Jordan retired, came back, retired, came back . . . and moved on to the Wizards! The pain of it all. With the announcement that the Field's candy kitchen was being shut down, 157 employees were suddenly without jobs. And the Windy City was losing a true Sweet Home Chicago original. But despite the appeals and even threats of the ever-irascible Mayor Daley, Field's charged ahead with its plans. You can either make a statement and boycott Frango, or, if you're like me, be a hypocrite and buy them anyway. They're that good. And over the years, the product line has grown to include other Frango goodies: Dark Mint, Toffee Crunch, Cookies 'N' Mint, Malted, Raspberry, and Praline Pecan.

If you're gripped by civic-duty guilt, **Belgian Chocolatier Piron** (509 Main Street, Evanston, 847-864-5504) will surely satisfy your sweet tooth. The bonbons, made from imported milk and dark Callebaut chocolate, are delectable. They come in all sorts of creative shapes, like seashells filled with chocolate hazelnut praline.

Margie's Candies (1960 North Western Avenue, 773-384-1035) is a family-run establishment dating all the way back to 1921. It's also a chocoholic's dream. Here you'll find old-fashioned confections like rich chunks of fudge, almond bark, and hand-dipped chocolate turtles loaded with caramel and pecans. You can even stand outside and watch through the windows as these heavenly goodies are made.

SECRET
CHRISTMAS

Andy Williams had it right — Christmas is "the most wonderful time of the year." I love Chicago during the holidays. Each year, on the Saturday before Thanksgiving, the **Magnificent Mile Lights Festival** draws thousands to watch the ceremonial lighting of, literally, hundreds of thousands of tiny white lights strung through the trees along Michigan Avenue. On the Friday after turkey day, the **Christmas Tree Lighting** at Daley Center Plaza is always a festive event. The tree, a gargantuan evergreen decorated with oversized ornaments, converts the plaza into an urban Christmas wonderland as tinny carols are piped over the public address system. Another bright display of holiday cheer is the **Zoo Lights Festival** at the Lincoln Park Zoo (2200 North Cannon Drive, 312-742-2000), held each season from late November through early January. Twinkling holiday lights are lit up all over the zoo in the shape of animals and dinosaurs. **Christmas around the World** (Museum of Science and Industry, 5700 South Lake Shore Drive, 773-684-1414) presents Christmas trees decorated in the traditional styles of more than 40 countries. Perhaps the grandest of Chicago holiday traditions are the windows at the **Marshall Field's** (111 North State Street, 312-781-1000) department store. Every year, this renowned Loop institution adorns the space behind the street-side display windows with a holiday theme, complete with moving characters and story line. Inside this grand shopping Mecca, which was designed by the famed Chicago architectural firm of D.H. Burnham and Company, families line up for and eat the best chicken potpie in the whole city under the lights of the towering Christmas tree in the Walnut Room.

SECRET
CLASSICAL

On a winter's night along Michigan Avenue, a dusting of swirling snow covers the sidewalk. Automobiles and buses slosh past under the cold glow of streetlamps. Inside the 98-year-old **Orchestra Hall** (220 South Michigan Avenue, 312-294-3000), the refrain of a Dvořák concerto performed by famed cellist Yo-Yo Ma reverberates within the newly restored and acoustically renovated space. This is just another magnificent night at the **Chicago Symphony Orchestra**.

Chicago's symphony is world renowned. Rewind to 1902. cso trustee and Chicago architect Daniel Burnham begins plans for what would become Orchestra Hall. The first concert takes place on December 14, 1904, under the baton of music director Theodore Thomas. Nine hundred albums and 53 Grammy Awards later, the Chicago Symphony Orchestra, now under the direction of Daniel Barenboim, is as strong as ever.

Perhaps you have a whole lot of cash to burn and a child prodigy in your house. If this is the case, well, you're damned lucky. You should pay a visit to **Bein & Fushi Rare Violins Incorporated** (410 South Michigan Avenue, 312-663-0150). Located on the top floor of the Fine Arts Building (see "Secret Architecture"), this 27-year-old store recently sold a Guarneri del Gesú built in 1737 for a measly $6 million. And this is all just in a day's work for owners Robert Bein and Geoffrey Fushi, whose store is the largest of its kind in the entire world. But this isn't just a high-end music shop. Geoff Fushi also runs the **Stradivari Society**, which persuades collectors of million-dollar violins to lend their instruments to master musicians. Fushi says that these violins, hand-crafted by Antonio Stradivari and Giuseppe Guarneri del Gesú, are not kept under glass but played, as they were meant to be.

Now that your little maestro has a multimillion-dollar violin, sign her up for the **Chicago Youth Symphony** (312-939-2207). This talented 112-piece orchestra is made up of the top-notch high school musicians in the Chicagoland area. They play many free concerts all over the city year round.

The **Chicago Music Mart** (333 South State Street, 312-362-6700) is well known for its free "Tunes at Noon" concerts. Almost every day during lunchtime, popular regional ensembles tune up and fill the lower lobby of the building with the sounds of strings, brass, and woodwinds. Recent performers include the **Classical Symphony Orchestra** (312-341-1521) and the **Newberry Consort** (312-943-9090). Consult one of the free schedules available at the Mart or contact the Music Mart for times. Some additional shows are offered in the evenings and on weekends.

Chicagoans who can afford it spend their summer evenings at the **Ravinia Festival** (Green Bay and Lake Cook Roads, Highland Park, 312-728-4642), which is half an hour north of downtown (in good traffic). Ravinia is an enormous outdoor music amphitheater with a pastoral scene of sloping hills, trees, and quiet little patches that you can stake out. Live symphonies, jazz artists, and an occasional adult-oriented rock band play under the covered pavilion. The Chicago Symphony Orchestra is a frequent guest at these sundown events, performing everything from lovers' concertos to Mozart medleys. But believe it or not, the enchanting music is just a soundtrack to the real reason people come to Ravinia — to picnic. Each night, families spread out blankets on the plush grass and set up shop. The crowd really goes all out, unpacking fine silverware, cloth napkins, and citronella candles. The meals are just as elaborate: fresh summer salads, fromage, chilled wine. Once the sun begins to set, the grassy knoll is aglow with candlelight and fireflies, and the airy sounds of the symphony fill the air, much to everyone's delight.

SECRET
CLUBS

For the uninitiated, the choices for clubbing are infinite: high fashion, high concept, techno, drum 'n' bass, boutique, retro, and hip-hop.

Here's a list of hot spots to help you sort it all out. But be fore-warned, the nightclub landscape is a constantly evolving nocturnal beast, with venues opening and closing quicker than a flash of heat lightning on the horizon. Clubs rely on trends and trends come and go. I've tried to pick spots that look like they'll be around for a long time, but don't come looking for me if a club has closed up shop.

The cavernous **Crobar** (1543 North Kingsbury Street, 312-413-7000) is, perhaps, the grand mammy of all Chicago dance clubs. On Friday nights inside this multi-tiered gothic industrial playground, you'll find the likes of big name national DJs like Moby or Keoko spinning discs. If your scene is drum 'n' bass, deep house, acid house, or techno, you've found the right place. And if you don't know what the hell any of that is, it doesn't matter. Crobar is a favorite with the gay commu-nity, celebrities, cross-dressers, and poseurs, which makes it a fabulous spot to people-watch. But be prepared to wait to get inside. The lines here put Disneyland to shame. And another tip — if you're driving, valet-park. The most maligned towing service in all of Chicago, Lincoln Park Towing, circles around this place in a ruthless feeding frenzy of unbridled greed.

Within the same uber-complex as Crobar, **Circus** (901 West Weed Street, 312-266-1200) is just one of many themed clubs in Chicago. Here you'll find a woman traversing a tightrope over the room while trendoids hobnob over high-priced cocktails. The **Dragon Room** (809 West Evergreen Avenue, 312-751-2900) is a three-level Japanese motif establishment with all-night dancing and a sushi bar. You'll find different styles of music on each tier. Bring your credit card and act like the high prices don't faze you a bit, and you'll fit right in. **Voyeur** (151 1/2 West Ohio Street, 312-832-1717) elevates the whole club culture mantra of "see or be seen" to new heights. There are several hidden video cameras perched throughout the club, but, of course, all you really see are people dancing badly. White-man's overbite, anyone?

Subterranean (2101 West North Avenue, 773-278-6600) is a good bet for low-key hip-hop grooves. One other plus: the crowd here, artists and college students, is refreshingly unpretentious. But if you really want to commingle with the dance community, head to the place serious house hounds and DJs go after hours. **Rednofive** (440 North Halsted Street, 312-733-6699) — pronounced "red number five" — blasts a wicked amalgam of techno and house beats. Saturday nights, this hipster haven stays open until 5 AM. At the **Liar's Club** (1665 West Fullerton Avenue, 773-665-1110), you can dance to the odd mix of Madonna one minute and KISS the next. You might also catch TV talk show sensationalist Jerry Springer and his bodyguards hanging out at the bar.

At **White Star** (225 West Ontario Street, 312-440-3223), the music is decidedly Top 40 dance. Don't forget your deodorant, please. Possibly the hottest club in town — but, remember, these trends come and go — is **Nocturnal** (1111 West Lake Street, 312-491-1931). Clothes are worn tight and chic and the techno tunes groove loud and proud. Even the so-called "lounge" areas are jam-packed and energetic.

SECRET

COFFEE

The major chains are very well represented in Chicago — Starbucks and Caribou Coffee shops are everywhere, near every elevated-train platform, on every street corner, by every Gap store. And mostly, the coffee is pricey and over-roasted while the prefab atmosphere is cloned and cold. At last count, there were more than 60 Starbucks in Chicago. Really, there's only one that's worth a visit — the one on Rush Street in the Gold Coast. On a cold winter's night, that **Starbucks** (932 North Rush Street, 312-951-5436) offers a crackling fire in the fireplace, deep sofas, and soft lighting. The atmosphere is surprisingly comfy. Still, the pretension inherent in most of these chain coffeehouses is as thick as a blueberry scone.

And then there are the little shops hidden away all over Chicago, like **Katerina's** (1920 West Irving Park Road, 773-348-7592). A few blocks from the Irving Park stop on the CTA Brown Line, this coffeehouse is a real oasis. The shop is darkly lit with plush, velvety sofas. It has live jazz, blues, and folk music playing every Wednesday through Saturday. Katerina's is a coffeehouse in the truest sense, where students and urbanites gather to write letters, talk politics, and read frayed paperbacks.

On a brilliant, sun-filled summer day, buy a cup of coffee at **Cafe Selmarie** (4729 North Lincoln Avenue, 773-989-5595) and then take a seat under a tree in the plaza outside. It's glorious.

If you're looking for some of the more chichi gourmet caffeinated concoctions minus the franchise, **Cafe Avanti** (3706 North Southport Avenue, 773-880-5959) is a great stop after a movie at the Music Box Theater (see "Secret Movies"). Its best cuppa is a kick-in-the-ass charge called the "Double Boris," (two blasts of deep-roasted espresso). Avanti also has regular exhibitions of local art, and there's a bowl of dog treats on the counter for your canine pal.

If you're in the Pilsen neighborhood, **Cafe Jumping Bean** (1439 West 18th Street, 773-455-0019) is a must stop. Wonderful local art adorns the walls and even the tables are hand-painted works to behold. This coffee haven reflects the alternative side of the Hispanic community that calls Pilsen home. **Bourgeois Pig** (738 West Fullerton Avenue, 773-883-JAVA) is a warm and relaxing retreat in the ultra-trendy Lincoln Park neighborhood. And while the coffee, along with an eclectic menu of soups and salads, is marvelous, be careful — parking in this area sucks.

On the far South Side, **Java Express** (10701 South Hale Street, 773-233-8557) is a great shop in the old working-class Beverly neighborhood. Situated on a narrow street, this establishment serves up some splendid joe along with a tasty array of tuna, veggie, turkey, and ham sandwiches, all priced between $4 and $5. Looking for beans? Java Express has around 20 blends. The most popular is the Beverly Blend, a rich mix of aromatic Colombian beans. The **Coffee & Tea Exchange** (3300 North Broadway Street, 773-528-2241) has a fine selection of locally roasted java — 20 roasts and 65 teas in all. Prices for coffee beans range from $6 to $9 a pound; tea is $9.95 pound. **Intelligentsia Coffee Roasters and Tea Blenders** (3123 North Broadway Street, 773-348-8058) carries a mother lode of beans roasted in the nearby Bucktown area. This is a real coffeehouse, where patrons are persuaded to sit as long as they wish, to chat, to ponder, to drink coffee, and to go to the bathroom about a hundred times due to that dreaded caffeine.

And last, but not least, there's **The Gossip Cafe** (12947 South Western Avenue, Blue Island, 773-653-5018), a charming, warm otherworld located just across the far South Side city limits in Blue Island. Here, you'll discover a friendly atmosphere and bottomless cups of coffee and tea, along with some mighty tasty morsels like sandwiches and pastries. The triple-decker peanut butter and jelly sandwich is a winner, as are the daily soups and the just-like-Mom-used-to-make homemade chili. Don't miss this place, but don't tell too many people about it either. You'll spoil the secret.

SECRET
COMEDY

The longevity of Chicago's comedy clubs is remarkable. But by now, everyone is well aware of the fact that **Second City** (1616 North Wells Street, 312-337-3992) was the training ground for a number of big-name celebs: John Belushi, Bill Murray, Alan Arkin, George Wendt, Gilda Radner, Chevy Chase, yada yada yada. Tell us something we didn't know. Right? Okay, while Second City — and for that matter, **Zanies** (1548 North Wells Street, 312-337-4027) — still toss out a good number of laughs, these places are like tourist roach motels, sucking in any out-of-towner with a wallet full of dough. The grassroots vibe of Second City is all but gone. And Zanies, with the exception of a few glimmers of comedic hope, is just for tourists who don't know where to go and for comedians fresh off a six-week run on a cruise ship. But we won't steer you astray. Here are the comedy stomping grounds of tomorrow.

If you laugh at raunchy humor, the **Annoyance Theatre** (3747 North Clark Street, 773-929-6200) has comedy that you will love. It's racy and it's raw. The popular *Coed Prison Sluts* has been running for over a decade with no end in sight. **Improv Olympic** (3541 North Clark Street, 773-880-0199) fires off long-form improv shows and sketch comedy with dead-on precision. Monday night is alumni night for many of the players who have moved on to Second City or the Annoyance. The **Hungry Brain** (2319 West Belmont Avenue,

773-929-6288) offers an open-mic improv on Sunday nights, hosted by the Second City Players workshop. It also has a splendid bar.

For family-friendly comedy (minimal profanity), check out **ComedySportz** (3209 North Halsted Street, 773-549-8080), where two improv teams square off in a battle royale.

SECRET
COMIC BOOKS

One of the biggest names in comic books today is Chicagoan Alex Ross. Ross's super-heroic artwork has catapulted him into the upper echelon of industry greats, prompting many to call him "the Norman Rockwell of comics." His incredibly realistic painting style caused a massive stir in 1993 with the release of the breathtaking Marvels. This four-issue mini-series chronicled the origins of Spiderman, Captain America, the Fantastic Four, et al., as if Stan Lee and Edward Hopper had spent a brainstorming weekend at a Wisconsin retreat. Ross's singular opaque watercolors are unparalleled in the field. So where does Alex Ross shop for comic books? **Chicago Comics** (3244 North Clark Street, 773-528-1983). Owner Eric Kirsammer, who also owns the very hip 'zine shop, Quimby's (see "Secret 'Zines"), has, according to Ross, "the best store in the entire Midwest." Organized, clean, and packed to the rafters with comics, toys, and other cool curios, Chicago Comics is a must-stop for all comic book fans.

Farther north, two worthy little ma and pa–style shops are **Galaxy Comic Zone** (3804 North Western Avenue, 773-267-1043) and **Variety Comics** (4602 North Western Avenue, 773-334-2550). Both of these stores are small, but they specialize in superhero books and have stockpiles of back issues.

S E C R E T
CURIOSITIES

You're never too old to take a class. Why not start piano lessons? Or how about learning a foreign language? You could get your scuba diving license or you could learn to fly an airplane. You could acquire a few sexy tango dance moves or you could try some of these even more obscure offerings.

Every Wednesday night around 6 PM, there's a powwow of sorts at **Native American Educational Services College** (2836 West Peterson Avenue, 773-761-5000) on the city's Northwest Side. In a classroom cluttered with desks and boxes, and Native American artwork placed crookedly on the walls, students gamely try to master a dying language — Lakota. For $180, you can join a 16-week course to learn the native tongue of the Sioux Indians. But don't say "dying language" around these parts. To the handful of students who take the class each semester, Lakota is alive and well. Why not audit the class and give it a try?

I have a beautiful old piano in my house, which was my mom's and her mom's before that. Whenever people come over, someone invariably remarks how he would love to learn to play a musical instrument, but it's too late. What is that? Like, when you hit 30 you can't learn? What crap. The **Old Town School of Folk Music** (4544 North Lincoln Avenue, 773-525-7793) is the place to start your musical journey. This

Chicago institution opened during the folk music boom of the late 1950s and early 1960s. The school flourished in the folkie '60s and then struggled in the electric '70s, but not before establishing itself by pumping out graduates like Steve Goodman, Roger McGuinn, Bonnie Koloc, and John Prine. The school rebounded stronger than ever with the rediscovery of acoustic and world music in the 1980s and 1990s. Today it has 20 classrooms, instructing more than 1,000 students weekly in everything from the fundamentals of guitar, banjo, and piano to Tahitian percussion. And it has a fabulous lineup of live music by top local, national, and even international folk acts in the 425-seat performance space.

Care to learn a few dance moves? Ballroom dancing is the craze these days. Try the **Chicago Ballroom and Studio** (3660 West Irving Park Road, 773-267-3411).

Columbia 2 (29 East Congress Parkway, 312-344-8190) is Columbia College's Division of Continuing Education. More and more people are pursuing continuing education to escape their humdrum day jobs. C2 offers a trove of affordable cool courses, including classes in art and design, Web page design, magazine writing, and sports and entertainment management.

SECRET
DELICATESSENS

Manny's Coffee Shop and Deli (1141 South Jefferson Street, 312-939-2855) is a South Side legend on the edge of downtown. Chicago aldermen power lunch in this vast, shabby, cafeteria-style delicatessen, where the sandwich to order is the mountainous corned beef. Two slicers work endlessly, peeling off three inches of layered meat that just barely wedges between the slices of rye. The place is always thronged with government desk jockeys, firemen, and prehistoric neighborhood old-timers. Grab a silver tray, load it up, and wait for a table to clear. With the enormity of the dining room, it usually doesn't take long.

Near Midway Airport is **Bobak's** (5275 South Archer Avenue, 773-735-5334), an enormous Polish delicatessen. It sells everything from kielbasa to veal sausage. You'll also find nasal passage–clearing horseradish and loaves of fresh-baked rye bread. Bobak's is a favorite with Chicago's Polish community, who come in for the buffet.

With posters of Mike Ditka, Al Capone, and Mayor Richard J. Daley hanging on the walls, **Finkl's World Famous Deli** (752 North Ogden Avenue, 312-829-1699) is a true Chicago-style deli. It's not gourmet deli, but what you'll get is comfort food like hot pastrami or chopped chicken liver sandwiches, which is okay with the busy lunchtime crowd. Finkl's does manage to put a spin on the artery-clogging deli diet by offering health-conscious lunches.

Here's a secret: Chicago's most affordably delicious deli food is found at the **White Hen Pantry.** Think of a squeaky clean 7-Eleven, and you get the picture. With locations throughout Chicagoland, this brightly lit superette has everything a mini-mart should: a big magazine rack, aisles of canned goods, candy, paper products, and fantastic deli sandwiches. A Genoa salami with pepper jack cheese, with a bag of chips and a soda, will run you about $5.

DOG FRIENDLY

Got a canine traveling companion? No problem. Chicago offers up plenty for your pooch. While Illinois state law prohibits dogs from entering establishments with food licenses, many taverns welcome your four-legged pal with a warm smile and a big bowl of cold water. There are even pooch-friendly al fresco restaurants, where you can leash your mutt up while you dine. But take it from me, dogs begging will not be tolerated! One Sunday afternoon, I carted my two little dust mops, Sage and Disney, into JT **Collins Pub** (3358 North Paulina Street, 773-327-7467) to watch a football game on the tube. JT's is one of those places that will occasionally let Fido inside, even with its food license. So I'm sitting at the bar, golden Weiss beer in hand, and I hear Sage barking at a table of young urbanites digging into a platter of nachos. Before I can even get over to the table, Sage, with her high-pitch wails, has everyone in the pub staring. The bartender summarily requests that we take a hike. "You're the only dog owner I've ever had to throw out," he says. Long story short — if you have a well-behaved dog, you're welcome in this watering hole, which features tasty pub grub. Try the flatbread with chicken sausage or, Sage's favorite, the nacho platter.

The **Ten Cat** (3931 North Ashland Avenue, 773-935-5377), a cozy North Side tavern, is very dog friendly. Come here enough and you're bound to run into regulars, human and canine. The most dog-friendly tavern in all of Chicago is the **Marquee Lounge** (1973 North Halsted Street, 312-988-7427), which always has a bowl of water, or treats if you ask, for your friend.

Whether you have a dog or not, **Rainbo Club** (1150 North Damen Avenue, 773-489-5999) is a cool bar for a pint of ale. The crowd is an eclectic mix of residents from the surrounding artsy Wicker Park neighborhood: painters, musicians, actors, poets, and students all come here for the good cheer and good beer. Dogs seem to like it too.

Looking for a restaurant with an al fresco section that will permit your pooch? Here are two of my favorites. **Club Creole** (226 West Kinzie Street, 312-222-0300), right behind the beautiful old Merchandise Mart, serves up great Cajun cuisine. Try the voodoo chicken — chicken stuffed with andouille sausage and a dollop of dirty rice on the side. **Once Upon a Thai** (3705 North Southport Avenue, 773-935-6433) has a low-key atmosphere and marvelous pad thai. My father loves the cucumber salad with peanut sauce dressing. On weekends, the restaurant features live zither music.

As for the best parks to run your pooch ragged, my dogs prefer "**Bark Park**," as it is unofficially known. It's located just south of Addison Street, on the lakefront. There's lots of open space for your pup to run around, and most people let their pals frolic off leash (even though it's technically illegal). Even on the coldest, most bitter January day, a regular cast of rambunctious canine characters can be found traipsing through the park. Just a little closer to Lake Shore Drive, off Recreation Drive, is **Dog Beach**, a small expanse of sand sloping into Belmont Harbor. Though the spot is just a few hundred feet of beachfront, it's cordoned off with a fence, so your best friend can jump in and out of the water and cavort with other pups with complete freedom. This is the city's most popular swimming retreat for local dogs. Personally, I don't bring my dogs here. The water is polluted and really quite gross. Rumor has it that many of the wealthy boaters who dock their yachts in nearby Belmont Harbor regularly dump the contents of their onboard toilets in the water. How nice. It's also funny how the cops patrolling this area are more concerned with nabbing pet owners for having their dogs off leash.

After years of carting my canine kids around town to various groomers, I discovered **City Groomers** (1407 West Irving Park Road, 773-832-4711). The twin sisters who own and operate this place are patient, loving, and gentle. A complete package that includes nail clipping, bath, shampoo, and cut runs around $38 per pet.

If you're looking for more ideas of things to do with your dog, Chicago author and radio talk show host **Steve Dale** has written a wonderful book called *Doggone Chicago*, published by Contemporary Books. You can also tune in to Dale's show, *Pet Central*, on WGN radio AM 720, Saturdays from 6 PM to 8 PM.

And finally, if you've ever seen the TV game show "The Price is Right," you are well familiar with Bob Barker's show-closing entreaty to spay or neuter your pets. Well, here's my Bob Barker spiel: if you have a little time or money and you love animals, then give PAWS (Pets Are Worth Saving) (1110 West 35th Street, 773-935-PAWS) a call. Founded in 1998, this nonprofit organization works tirelessly to establish Chicago as a no-kill city by finding homes for all adoptable pets. More than 35,000 cats and dogs are destroyed each year in the US, and, sadly, Chicago has one of the highest kill rates. It is PAWS's mission to save them all. The organization works as an adoption agency for many local shelters, placing thousands of animals in loving homes. It also operates its own **Cat Adoption Center** (2337 North Clark Street, 773-935-PAWS) and offers a low-cost spay/neuter clinic.

End of public service announcement.

S E C R E T
EL
☙

To an outsider, Chicago's public transportation system can be confusing, stressful, and even maddening. But really, once you get the hang of it — and this comes quickly — you realize how simple and comprehensive the Chicago Transit Authority's program really is. The elevated train, or the El, as we like to call it, is a symbol of our city. Late afternoons, with the sun setting, it snakes all silvery gold through nearly every part and pocket of town. The El goes just about everywhere. It carries home hordes of rush-hour workers from downtown. It rumbles out to O'Hare and Midway airports. It crackles over side streets and alleyways to communities north and south, large and small, rich and poor, black and white. In an era of racial profiling, gay-bashing, and the rich getting richer and the poor getting poorer, the elevated train connects a city that can sometimes feel disconnected.

The El first appeared in 1893, transporting passengers to the World's Columbian Exposition, on a three-and-a-half-mile length of track that ran from Congress Boulevard to 39th Street. Today, trains run on 289 miles of track serving 140 stations all over Chicago.

First, let's cover some safety issues. After living more than half of my life in Chicago, I've never had a problem riding the train. This is not to say that incidents don't occur, but common sense prevails. I was mugged once in Los Angeles. Why? Because my Chicago mouth flapped off to guys bigger than me. After a nasty ass-whuppin', I've learned when to keep my mouth shut. It's called street smarts. Stick around crowds. Don't ride the El late at night all alone through the more obscure neighborhoods. Don't display a Rolex watch or

Grandma's six-carat diamond hand-me-down. When boarding a train, don't fidget around in the doorway. The doors will whisk shut and you'll be trapped. This actually happened to one of my very best friends. His foot was stuck between the concrete platform and the train. He ended up losing his leg on that sad summer night. Fortunately, he's doing just fine today. But the moral of the story is to use your head. Be street smart and you'll be fine.

When you set out, you'll want a CTA transit map in hand. It's free and you can grab one at many El stations, as well as at the CTA's main office at the Merchandise Mart (350 North Wells Street) and the office at 181 West Madison Street. You can reach CTA customer assistance at 836-7000 (no area code necessary). Schedules are also posted online at www.transitchicago.com.

There are only five train lines. Each one is designated by a color and a name. All you really need to remember is the color and you'll be fine. The color of each is displayed in the window above the train operator, as well as in windows on the side of the train. All lines at some point return to the downtown area.

The **Red Line (Howard/Dan Ryan)** runs from Howard Avenue on the northern edge of the city, all the way south to 95th and State. This line takes you to both Major League ballparks, **Wrigley Field** (Addison stop) and **Comiskey Park** (35th Street stop). It also goes underground through downtown, where it makes a number of stops. And let's be honest here — because, after all, this book is not a public relations tool for the Office of Mayor Richard M. Daley: some areas, particularly around Comiskey Park, which is near the Robert Taylor Homes housing projects, should be avoided late at night. Just play it smart.

If you want to get back and forth from **O'Hare International Airport** (O'Hare stop), the **Blue Line (O'Hare Congress/Douglas)** is your train. It also goes through the trendy Wicker Park area along the way (Damen stop).

To get to **Midway Airport**, take the **Orange Line (Midway)**. This is a nice, quick run that should take no longer than 30 minutes from downtown. The **Green Line (Lake-Jackson Park/Englewood)** serves the West Side and South Side of the city. On the West, it starts in Oak Park (Harlem stop) and travels through downtown before heading south to 63rd Street (Ashland/63rd stop). More common sense on the southern run is advised after hours. For a tour of several of the city's ethnic neighborhoods, the **Brown Line (Ravenswood)** is a good bet. This train takes you north from downtown through the predominantly German Lincoln Square area (Western stop) to the Korean pocket (Kimball stop).

It costs $1.50 to ride the El (or the bus). For 30 cents more, you can transfer two more times to a different bus or train line, as long as you do so within two hours. After that, it's full fare again. This is a lot of hopping around in two hours' time. It's likely you won't switch this often, but in case you do, don't go buying new fares for a buck fifty with each ride.

The CTA uses magnetic transit cards that you can purchase from machines at any station. They are reusable, so you can keep adding as much money on them as you'd like. If you switch lines, the machine automatically registers whether you are a new rider or transferring. Keep your card.

And here's a money-saving hint: you can transfer on several downtown train lines without paying the additional 30 cents. Certain stations allow free transfers where you step off one train and climb aboard another. You don't go through a turnstile and you don't get charged. If you want to dash all over Chicago for the least amount of dough, this is the way to do it.

Another way to save a few bucks is to purchase a visitor pass. For example, a one-day pass is $5 for unlimited rides. A five-day pass with unlimited rides is $18. If you will be taking the train a lot, this is your best deal.

S E C R E T
EROTICA

Chicago is by no means a shy town. When it comes to our sports teams, we are loud and proud. On our freeways, we let you know what we think with our horns and with our fingers. Our politics are heated. Our leaders are opinionated and sometimes just plain crass. But when it comes to sex, Chicago blushes. Perhaps it's our old-fashioned heartland roots coming through. To most Windy City residents, sex is a private thing done behind closed doors. There is no red light district in Chicago. No long stretch of nightshade neon flashing "Triple xxx." No concentration of peep shows. No center for sex shops. But you can find all of this and more — it's just scattered.

The big-name porn stars who are touring the country and doing pitiable dance routines — just rolling around on the floor naked and calling it "striptease" — perform at the **Admiral Theatre** (3940 West Lawrence Avenue, 312-478-8263). The days of the burlesque houses, when strippers approached their craft as art, are long gone. Long gloves, bubble machines, and ostrich feathers have been replaced by smut, silicone implants, and a get-your-panties-off-ASAP mentality. 'Tis a shame. Still, this 24,000-square-foot sex complex is open until 4 AM, Monday through Saturday, and stays open until 3 AM on Sundays for near round-the-clock jollies. A sex shop inside the theater sells all sorts of deviant wares, including a large selection of porn videos. But the biggest downer — no booze. Who the hell wants to have an uninhibited evening without a little alcohol to loosen things up?

At the **Crazy Horse Too** (1531 North Kingsbury Street, 312-664-7400), an upscale gentleman's club, booze is plentiful. More than 200 showgirls on the payroll perform continuous stage shows and kinky lap dances.

Ladies looking for a night out on the town or a bachelorette party that includes manly entertainment will have to book a private male stripper. Furthering the notion that Chicago is sex-shy, there are no male strip clubs in the Windy City. Consult the *Chicago Reader's* classified section for a plethora of endowed dudes (see "Secret Periodicals"). You can also call the **One of a Kind** entertainment agency (312-464-9009), a local booking agency that provides both male and female strippers. Here, you'll find guys with names like "Big Jim" and "Magnum" at your beck and call. Prices run from $95 for a 20-minute G-string routine to $125 for half an hour of uninhibited beefcake.

Every big metropolis has its lion's share of adult toy stores. Chicago is no exception. The best of the lot is **Cupid's Treasure** (3519 North Halsted Street, 773-348-3884) and its annex, **Cupid's Leather** (3503 North Halsted Street, 773-868-0914). Inside these dark caves of debauchery, you'll find all sorts of nasty and naughty lingerie, sex toys/power tools, magazines, riding crops, oils, lubes, brass balls for places where the sun don't shine, porno videos, and leather outfits that would make Cher blush.

ETHNIC BAKERIES

With such ethnic diversity, Chicago, not surprisingly, offers a wide selection of bakeries that reflect its different cultures. At the **Swedish Bakery** (5348 North Clark Street, 773-561-8919) in the quaint, leafy Andersonville neighborhood, a wealth of very reasonably priced delectable goodies awaits you. But sometimes the selection of mouth-watering confections is simply overwhelming. The chocolate raspberry buttercream cake is always scrumptious. And the apple walnut coffee cake makes for a perfect Sunday-morning snack.

Certainly you would do just fine walking into any of the bakeries scattered along West Devon Avenue near Western Avenue. Try **Casablanca Bakery** (1541 West Devon Avenue, 773-764-7482) for the ambrosial sweet olive loaves, poppyseed rolls, and other Persian delights.

Established in 1908, **Ferrara's Original Bakery** (2210 West Taylor Street, 312-666-2200) is the oldest Italian pastry shop in Chicago. And after all this time, it's got the baking down to a science. Try the amaretto cookies or the marzipan to satisfy that sweet tooth. Still not satisfied? Then make a run for the Iranian **Pars Persian Store** (5260 North Clark Street, 773-769-6635) for the flaky, scrumptious baklava.

Just a few blocks north of where I lived for many years is **Balingit Bakery, Inc.** (4019 North Damen Avenue, 773-477-6806), a Filipino establishment with a small but near-perfect selection of treats that are buttery and bready and dusted with sugar. Hopia is a safe bet. It's like nutty cookies with a sugary zing. And for a taste of gay Paris, **Sweet Thang** (1921 West North Avenue, 773-772-4166) has glass-fronted

shelves chock-full of tempting tarts: lemon, raspberry, pecan, chocolate, and apricot. The shop also bakes up airy croissants and cookies and cakes.

SECRET
FAST FOOD

The cloned franchises of the world have nothing on the ma and pa joints that symbolize true fast food Americana. These aren't your typical hot dog stands, mind you. We're talking a veritable cornucopia of fat friendly foods served on red plastic lunch trays. Mouth-watering char-burgers. All-beef hot dogs loaded with the works. Piping hot pizza puffs. Thick and chilly milk shakes and, of course, grease-glistening onion rings. Chicago has plenty of these special places all over town. After all, we're a city of big shoulders and even bigger beer guts. Most of these fast-food joints are scattered throughout the working-class pockets of the city. Only the longtime locals know about these places — the kind of establishments that sponsor the local Little League baseball team.

Man-Jo-Vin's (3224 North Damen Avenue, 773-935-0727), for a fast-food joint, is a bit pricey and the hired help can be, to put it kindly, a bit grouchy. But oh, the food. The Italian beef sandwiches, loaded with melted cheese and hot or sweet sport peppers, are some of the best to be found in the city. And as long as we're on the subject, **Al's #1 Italian Beef** (1079 West Taylor Street, 312-733-8896), in the heart of Little Italy, takes credit for inventing the Italian beef sandwich. This 62-year-old establishment has reached near mythical stature for its great chow and great old-time neighborhood vibe.

Gyro lovers need to go no further than **Rainbow Drive In** (4136 North Western Avenue, 773-478-3838). Buy a gyro for $5.99 and feed two people, but ask for extra pita bread. These sandwiches are overstuffed and outstanding. Another sure bet at this tiny roadside shack are the cooked-to-perfection char-burgers.

But if I have to choose one joint as the best, it's **Anthony's** (4720 West 63rd Street, 773-585-7180). Hidden in a blue-collar Polish neighborhood just at the end of a Midway Airport runway, Anthony's is a favorite of locals and airport employees. Summer nights in the parking lot, with the window down and Boeing 737s coming in with their wheels outstretched, are the time to chow down and listen to a ballgame on the radio. You want Americana? This is it. Anthony's serves up fabulous golden onion rings, terrific burgers, pizza puffs, beef sandwiches, and absolutely incredible milkshakes. The pineapple shake is made with fresh chunks of fruit so big they get lodged in your straw. Anthony's also offers fresh salads and superb barbecue rib tips. It's no wonder this place is always jam packed.

S E C R E T
FEMINISM

The front lines of feminism in Chicago can be found at **Women & Children First** (5233 North Clark Street, 773-769-9299), a 22-year-old independent bookstore devoted to all things female. From Madonna to motherhood, owners Linda Bubon and Ann Christopherson have cultivated a creative and literary Mecca for readings, children's events, book clubs, and semi-political powwows. The shop hosts an average of 12 to 15 events a month, including visits by the biggest women writers in literature: Amy Tan, Joyce Carol Oates, Toni Morrison, and Jane Hamilton. "What I love about their store," says Hamilton, whose novel, *The Book of Ruth*, was one of the early Oprah Winfrey book club selections, "is that there is an intelligence behind their choices of books. When you walk in, every book is a book that you want to read." With a huge selection of feminist books and magazines, as well as children's storytime each Wednesday morning from 10:30 AM to 11 AM for kids aged two to four, this is the place for Grrl power.

S E C R E T
FOREIGN VIDEO

Chicago comprises 77 distinct neighborhoods. Many of them were established in the 19th century by immigrants: Poles, Germans, Irish, and Jews. Even after 150 years, Chicago's ethnic enclaves are still very distinct. Walk the streets of Ukrainian Village and you will hear old ladies sitting on front porches speaking in their native tongue. Visit the Ravenswood area and you will encounter groups of Germans attending church together or polka dancing in one of the area's many German restaurants. And in each of these separate urban nooks, you will spot a video store that caters to the local culture — keeping people connected to their homelands through film.

Huan Thu (4820 North Broadway Street, 773-784-4433) is like many shops in the Uptown neighborhood. It carries a little bit of everything. Many of the stores along the main drag in Uptown have window displays loaded with shoes, T-shirts, wooden carvings, and porcelain statuettes. In the rear of Huan Thu, a counter is stocked

with Vietnamese videos. And the prices beat Blockbuster's by a mile
— to rent a video, it's 80 cents a day.

Bollywood, India's film industry, is the world's busiest, churning out
nearly 800 movies a year. **Atlantic Video** (2541 West Devon Avenue,
773-338-3600) stocks the largest inventory of Bollywood titles in the
city, with a strong selection of classics dating back to the 1930s.
Atlantic has an impressive number of art films, too. The store is
well lit and the movies are displayed like Blockbuster's, with the
boxes out on shelves. You'll also find a trough of Indian soundtracks.
Al-Mansoor (2600 West Devon Avenue, 773-764-7576) is also well
stocked with Bollywood titles on video and DVD.

Chinese Video Express (1139 West Argyle Street, 773-878-2914) is
always packed with customers who speak neither Cantonese nor
Mandarin, thanks in large part to the success of legendary director
John Woo and the Hong Kong action genre in general.

Bodak Video (3248 North Pulaski Avenue, 773-777-3129) caters to
Chicago's very large Polish population. And while the selection isn't
massive, it does stock several Chicago-produced Polish-language films.

SECRET

FRANK LLOYD WRIGHT

Just on the fringe of the Chicago city limits is the green town of Oak
Park, Illinois. It was here that one of America's most illustrious architects, Frank Lloyd Wright, auspiciously catapulted his reputation.
Without question, the 20 years Wright spent in Oak Park firmly
put his name on the map. They also indelibly changed Chicago's

architectural aesthetic. While the **Frank Lloyd Wright Home and Studio** (951 Chicago Avenue, 708-848-1976) offers an extraordinary tour showcasing the genesis of an architectural genius, most people don't go beyond this landmark. There are many Wright masterpieces scattered about town that you can't tour, but that are worth a drive-by.

First, let me play tour guide with a somewhat tragic sidebar. Despite his notoriety, one out of every five of Wright's buildings — more than 100 structures worldwide — has been destroyed. Some were demolished, others decimated by fires and neglect.

In Oak Park, Wright's work is most concentrated along Forest Avenue, running from Chicago Avenue south to Ontario Street. Seven homes on this stretch are by Wright. Can you guess which ones? I leave it up to you.

One of Wright's more impressive small home designs is on a little cul-de-sac that veers off Forest Avenue about halfway down the thoroughfare. The **Mrs. Thomas H. Gale House** (6 Elizabeth Court, Oak Park) was built in 1909, and most scholars of the architect recognize this design to be a precursor to Wright's renowned Fallingwater. The **Winslow House** (515 Auvergne Place, Oak Park), built in 1894, was Wright's first independent commission. What you'd learn on the tour of Oak Park (that you would have paid for, but I'm telling you instead) is that this design is highly reminiscent of fellow Chicago architect Louis Sullivan's style.

Wright was known for creating what is called the Prairie School of architecture. These designs emphasized low-pitched roofs and long horizontal lines. The windows often had abstract, geometric ornamentation. The walls were flat brick or stucco, often outlined with wooden strips of contrasting color. Wright drew inspiration for this style from the plains west of Chicago, and in doing so, he created a new form of American architecture. The house that many think best exemplifies the Prairie style is the **Coonley House** (300 Scottswood, Riverside). While overcrowding in the surrounding neighborhood has compromised the original design, this is still an impressive place to visit.

While he didn't design the building, Frank Lloyd Wright left an enduring impression on the **Rookery Building** (209 South LaSalle Street) in downtown Chicago. This structure was designed by Burnham and Root — famous architects in their own right. But in 1905, Wright came in and remodeled the large sky-lit lobby, introducing elements characteristic of his Prairie School designs. It's a stunner.

Wright called **Robie House** (5757 South Woodlawn Avenue, 708-848-1976), in the Hyde Park neighborhood, his best design. By the time the house was built in 1910, the architect had perfected the Prairie style. With its powerful limestone sills and overhanging roofs, the horizontal layout exemplifies Wright's quest to reflect the tableland of the American Midwest. Today, it is occupied by the University of Chicago's Office of Alumni Affairs. The house is open daily for one-hour tours.

And one last bit of trivial fodder. Did you know that Wright's son, John, designed the popular Lincoln Log toys? It's true.

SECRET
GARDENS

The **Chicago Botanic Garden** (1000 Lake Cook Road, Glencoe, 847-835-5440) is 385 acres of total tranquility. There are 23 specialty gardens, including a wondrous English walled garden, dark and deep in foliage. Then there's the Japanese island garden, with wooden bridges and trickling waterfalls and, of course, bonsai trees. In 2000, a bonsai master from Japan contributed more than 20 rare bonsais to the Botanic Garden, making the collection one of the largest in the country. Another less trafficked spot in the park is the Suzanne S. Dixon Tallgrass Prairie. This expanse is simply stunning, but most visitors miss it because it's the farthest point from the entrance. Look hard for it on the general map, which barely acknowledges it. Still, this isolated realm is a beautiful snapshot of what Illinois once was — natural prairie. Weekends get a bit crowded at the Botanic Garden, with wedding parties unloading by the dozens for pristine photo opportunities. But a mid-week visit affords the perfect spot for a picnic or a peaceful stroll. Teeming with flowers and trees — 1.2 million plants in all — this retreat would definitely be on my top-10 list of "best places in Chicago," if I had such a list. You can find out more at the garden's Web site at www.chicago-botanic.org.

Another beautiful botanical hideaway, 45 minutes west of downtown, is **Cantigny** (1 South 151 Winfield Road, Wheaton, 630-668-5161). This park was once the estate of *Chicago Tribune* editor and publisher Colonel Robert R. McCormick, who died in 1955. He left the property to be maintained as a recreational and educational park. The juxtaposition of colorful flower thickets against hulking old tanks from World War II is a bit strange but, after all, McCormick was a veteran of the World War I and even named his property after a battlefield he fought on. The old mansion is now a comprehensive military museum — the **First Division Museum**, dedicated to McCormick's division, the famous "Big Red One."

Closer to the city are two magnificent conservatories open from 9 AM to 5 PM every day of the year, free of charge. The **Lincoln Park**

Conservatory (2400 North Stockton Drive, 312-742-7529) is a lush, tropical three-acre paradise. There's a palm house, overgrown with exotic greenery, as well as a fernery and cactus house. Seasonal flower shows are presented throughout the year. Call for schedules. Outside the conservatory each spring, when robins hop across a damp and spongy Lincoln Park foraging for worms, you'll find a symphony of nearly 20,000 flowers budding and blooming and popping.

The **Garfield Park Conservatory** (300 North Central Park Avenue, 312-746-5100) is one of Chicago's best-kept secrets. Just 15 minutes west of downtown, it sees far less traffic than its sister conservatory in trendy Lincoln Park. Built between 1906 and 1907, Garfield Park is the largest enclosed horticultural facility in the world. While the 5,000 plants are cool, the architecture (of both the conservatory and the surrounding park) is the real belle of the ball. Designed by landscape architect Jens Jensen, in collaboration with Prairie School architects, the simple yet powerful structure was built to emulate the haystacks of the Midwest and complement the vast collection of plants housed within.

As the North Side of the city is gentrified, the South Side is increasingly becoming the place with the real, secret retreats. One such hideaway is the **Osaka Garden** (on Wooded Island in Jackson Park, 6401 South Stony Island, 312-747-6187). This authentic Japanese garden was originally constructed by the Japanese government as part of the 1893 World's Columbian Exposition. It features a replica of the Phoenix Temple near Kyoto, Japan, and has footbridges and all the flowers and rocks and shrubbery one might find while in the Land of the Rising Sun. A meditative rock waterfall was added during a 1981 renovation.

Known only by its neighbors, **Sunken Gardens Park** (4500 North Virginia Avenue, no phone) is situated on a sliver of land off the

Chicago River. Hidden away in the shady Ravenswood Manor neighborhood, this tiny public park is quiet and serene — the perfect spot to sit and think. Just a few blocks east, the **Waters Community Park** (4540 North Campbell Avenue, 773-534-5090) is unique to Chicago. More than a decade ago, Tom Revollo, the principal at Waters Elementary School, dreamed of having a community garden on the playground of his school. He hoped that the garden could be an integral part of the educational process — integrating ecology, geology, and an appreciation of art and nature. With help from ecologist Pete Leki, Revollo's dream became a reality. Today, Waters Garden plays a major role in the students' lives. Neighbors in the community have also contributed to the garden. Twenty-three separate families have planted a thicket of vegetables that includes tomatoes, cucumbers, green peas, squash, and even green chilies. There is also tall-grass prairie, left to grow wild, that birds love.

SECRET
GOD

Conservative estimates figure that Chicago has around 2,000 churches. Just take a look while driving down any of the expressways and you will wonder if perhaps there may be more. The entire cityscape is dotted by steeples and spires and domes. Many of these architectural wonders are simply the most beautiful buildings in the entire city — stretching toward the heavens in Gothic splendor. But you need not have religious convictions or affiliations to appreciate these marvels. Simply wander in and behold.

St. Mary's of the Angels (1850 North Hermitage Avenue, 773-278-2644) is the largest Roman Catholic church in Illinois. It's also one of the most beautiful. Measuring 230 feet by 125, St. Mary's has 32 nine-foot angels perched around the parapet. At night they're highlighted by bright spotlights. Walk into St. Mary's any afternoon in the middle of the week and you may just be all alone in a space that holds 1,800. Sit back in one of the pews and look straight up. The tile and terra-cotta dome was built to look like Michelangelo's masterpiece at St. Peter's Basilica in Vatican City.

In the Ukrainian Village, a quiet pocket inhabited by immigrants, artists, and students, is **St. Nicholas Ukrainian Catholic Cathedral** (2338 West Rice Street, 773-276-4537). Modeled after the multi-domed, 11th-century Cathedral of St. Sophia in Kiev, St. Nicholas is washed in blue and gold light that filters through its stunning stained-glass windows. The nine-tiered chandelier, boasting 480 lights, is said to be the largest of its kind in the country.

The **Fourth Presbyterian Church** (126 East Chestnut Street, 312-787-4570) stands at odds with the flurry of fur coats, flawless diamonds, and pricey designer shops all around it on the Mag Mile. But once you walk into the ivy-paved courtyard, you enter a world of tranquility — sort of an eye of the metropolitan hurricane. The **Second Presbyterian Church** (1936 South Michigan Avenue, 312-225-4951) gets the nod for the best stained-glass windows in a Chicago church. At one time, the surrounding neighborhood, known as the Prairie Avenue district, was the Beverly Hills of Chicago. All the Windy City royalty lived here. The Fields. The Shaws. The Armours. All this money purchased renowned architect James Renwick, who designed New York's St. Patrick's Cathedral. Built in 1874 after the original Renwick-designed structure at Washington and Wabash was destroyed in the Chicago Fire, this beautiful house of worship boasts nine name-brand Tiffany windows. From the *Pastoral Window* on the northwest corner, with its brilliant hues of pinks and blues and greens, to *The Ascension* on the east wall — a four-ton masterpiece four inches thick in some spots — these visions of light are well worth a Sunday visit.

At the **Bultasa Buddhist Temple** (4360 West Montrose Avenue, 773-286-1551), you'll find the largest number of Buddha figures on any altar in the Midwest — one thousand in all. For really impressive, really ornate stained glass, walk into the **Lake Shore Drive Synagogue** (70 East Elm Street, 312-337-6811). Constructed in 1953, the **Baha'i House of Worship** (100 Linden Avenue, Wilmette, 847-853-2300) is well worth the half-hour trek north from downtown Chicago. Right near the water's edge, overlooking Lake Michigan and rising 191 feet in the air, this majestic temple has four stories of lace-like concrete rounding toward the top. There are nine sides to the building, each with an entrance. Architectural styles and symbols from many faiths are subtly incorporated into the design, which reflects the Baha'i faith by celebrating all the world's religions.

For yet more stunning stained-glass art, visit the **Chicago Loop Synagogue** (16 South Clark Street, 312-346-7370). Here you will find a masterful 30-by-40-foot wall of cosmic and Hebraic symbolism entitled *Let There Be Light, And There Was Light*, designed by American artist Abraham Rattner.

Moving on in our whirlwind tour of beautiful Chicago houses of worship: no travel guide, no matter how "secret," would be complete without mentioning Frank Lloyd Wright's **Unity Temple** (875 West Lake Street, Oak Park 708-383-8873). Construction began on the building in 1906, with Wright hoping to turn conventional church architecture on its ear. Visit the church and you will find that he succeeded in a big, bold way. There's no steeple, no spires, no bell tower. This stark concrete building with high-positioned stained-glass windows and bright, spacious interiors is yet one more bit of proof that Wright was a revolutionary with class. The building was named in 1970 to the National Register of Historic Places.

S E C R E T

GRAVEYARDS

Cemeteries are not just places to inhume the dead. They are urban nature preserves. They are home to myriad wildlife, like squirrels, opossums, raccoons, and birds. They can teach you about architecture, with their ornate granite headstones, lonesome statuary, and looming mausoleums. They can teach you about an area's history — about its earliest settlers, its war veterans, and its people of high repute. They are also a domain of emotion — a far-off figure kneels at a grave; a potted plant withers, left on a Mother's Day past.

A short distance north of Wrigley Field is **Graceland Cemetery** (4001 North Clark Street, 773-525-1105), a tranquil retreat for an introspective afternoon stroll. It's one of the city's more fascinating graveyards. Many of Chicago's rich and famous rest here. Before the Chicago Park District established its network of parks, Graceland was a popular spot for Chicagoans to get away from it all. Take a trek and look for the graves of architect Louis Sullivan, retailer Marshall Field, railcar tycoon George Pullman, Chicago city planner Daniel Burnham, and famed architect Mies van der Rohe.

Civil War buffs will want to visit **Rosehill Cemetery** (5800 North Ravenswood Street, 773-561-5940), where 16 war generals and

230 Union soldiers are buried. This 350-acre expanse is a bona fide nature retreat. Explore just a bit and you may also discover the graves of mail-order king Aaron Montgomery Ward, philanthropist and former Marshall Field president John G. Shedd, and 15 Chicago mayors. You can also pay respects to shoe czar Milton Florsheim and weenie magnate Oscar Mayer. The city's oldest graveyard, **Oak Woods Cemetery** (1035 East 67th Street, 773-288-3800), is another burial ground steeped in Civil War history. Six thousand Confederate soldiers, who died while imprisoned at Camp Douglas, are buried here. Other Chicago luminaries include Mayor Harold Washington, Olympic medalist Jesse Owens, and Enrico Fermi, the father of the atomic bomb.

Not many people know that Jack Ruby, the man who greased Lee Harvey Oswald before he could tell his side of the JFK assassination story, is buried in Chicago. You can visit Jack's grave in **Westlawn Cemetery** on the Northwest Side (7801 West Montrose Avenue, 773-625-8600). Film critic Gene Siskel was also buried here in 1999.

Okay, pop-culture cemetery secret: Robert Reed, better known as Mike Brady from "The Brady Bunch," was laid to rest at **Memorial Park Cemetery** (5225 Old Orchard Road, Skokie, 847-663-1039).

SECRET
HAMBURGERS

For over 30 years, **Moody's Pub** (5910 North Broadway Street, 773-275-2696) has been a favorite with Chicagoans for serving charcoal-grilled half-pound burgers teetering on the brink of being unwieldy. You can taste the smoke from the grill with each bite. These are big burgers, perfectly and evenly charred — a rare feat in the realm of the monster-sized hamburger. In the winter, a fire crackles in the dining room. And in the summer . . . well, just take a look at "Secret Al Fresco" for details on one of the city's best outdoor restaurant retreats. Weighing in even heavier on the scale is the one-pound brick served at **Capital Grille** (633 North St. Clair Street, 312-337-9400), where the secret isn't the size, it's the ground onion and bacon mixed in with the sirloin.

I'm dumbfounded as to why I'm recommending this place twice in the same book (see "Secret Beer Gardens"), when it ranks as one of Chicago's most annoying and crowded establishments come weekends. Frat boys jostling for women is a bad scene, indeed. But weeknights, when the crowd is thin, **John Barleycorn Memorial Pub** (658 West Belden Avenue, 773-348-8899) is very enjoyable, and it serves one of the best burgers in town. For burger purists, it's a perfect, flavorful half-pounder. For the avant-garde, there's an assortment of optional toppings, like Roquefort cheese, green olives, and guacamole. And one more plus about this place: mobster John Dillinger was a regular back in the speakeasy days. At the **Twisted Spoke** (501 North Ogden Avenue, 312-666-1500), the aptly named "fatboy" — a juicy burger in a garlic toasted bun — is a big hit. Top it with BBQ sauce, bacon, and grilled onions and make sure you cut it in half — how do you think this thing got its name?

SECRET

HANGOVER CURES

There are three avenues of thinking when it comes to overindulging. The first is prevention. **Sherwyn's** (645 West Diversey Avenue, 773-477-1934), arguably the city's finest health food store (see "Secret Wellness"), sells milk thistle. Supposedly, milk thistle coats the liver and protects it as you do your barroom battle.

The second train of thought is to give your system sustenance. When the partying is over and you are completely and totally schnookered, the oldest trick in a Chicagoan's book is to stop at a **White Castle**, which has several locations scattered about the city. This late-night fast-food joint is well known for its "sliders" — greasy little square burgers, steam cooked and loaded with minced onions. And they're cheap. You can buy a sack of 10 (they're small) for just $4.20 plus tax.

Finally, what do you do when you wake up feeling like shit? Two words: greasy spoons. Chicago has several restaurants sure to get you over the hump and, if you're lucky, back out on the playing field the very next day. Serving up scalding-hot, cast-iron skillets piled high with diced potatoes, melted cheese, bell peppers, onions, and chorizo, the **Lincoln Restaurant** (4008 North Lincoln Avenue, 773-248-1820) provides a fine start to any morning that begins with the mantra "I'm never gonna drink again." The skillets' historic names — such as the Merrimac and the Monitor — help lend you the resolve to combat the civil war progressing in your stomach. When you're dehydrated and bedraggled, the Lincoln welcomes you. And the dark wood paneling goes easy on bloodshot eyes.

Another one of my favorite coffee shops that offers terrific breakfast chow for the crapulent crowd is **Lakeview** (3243 North Ashland Avenue, 773-525-5695). Nothing fancy here, and certainly no view of Lake Michigan. But you will find good quarter-pound hamburger patties topped with two eggs over easy, giant Greek omelettes stuffed with onion, tomato, and feta cheese, and a long menu of other tasty breakfast options. By the way, the lunch and dinner menu here is just as fine. And the people-watching is pretty spectacular as well. The surrounding neighborhood is an eclectic amalgam of cell phone–yapping yups, pontificating college art students, and elderly folks who live in the nearby YMCA.

S E C R E T
HEALTH CLUBS

Traveling can really throw a daily fitness regimen out of whack. And unless you belong to a chain with a network of health clubs across the country, you need to find workout alternatives. Most of my out-of-town friends love to jog or blade along Chicago's lakefront. The paved path runs between Lake Shore Drive and the lake from **Kathy Osterman Beach** (Ardmore Avenue, 5800 North and the lake) on the north to the **South Shore Cultural Center** (7059 South Shore Drive, 312-747-2536) on the south. This is always one way to get some exercise. But let's be realistic — in January, when the average low is a crisp 18 degrees Fahrenheit, who the hell wants to jog?

Eschewing the mirrors, neon, and beefcake bravado of most franchise health clubs, the **New City YMCA** (1515 North Halsted Street, 312-266-1242) offers a pleasant reprieve from the narcissistic thong nation. With an Olympic-sized swimming pool and all the latest workout machines for $10 a day, an out-of-towner can stay fit. You can become a member of the Y for $100 down and $35 a month. Classes in all sorts of hip things, like fencing, yoga, and cardio boxing, are available for an additional fee. The **Lincoln-Belmont YMCA** (3333 North Marshfield Avenue, 773-248-3333) is an even better daily deal, with $8-per-day fees for guests. The only catch — nonmembers can only work out Friday through Sunday if they are accompanied by an active Y member, in which case you can go to town all week long.

For women who want to escape the probing eyes of gross gawkers, **Women's Workout World**, with five locations (208 South LaSalle, 312-357-0001; 2540 West Lawrence Avenue, 773-334-7341; 5030 South Kedzie Avenue, 773-434-8900; 5201 South Harper Avenue, 773-684-3000; 1031 North Clark Street, 312-664-2106), is the answer. This fitness center sports plenty of state-of-the-art machinery and it is a chicks-only affair.

SECRET
HERB

Dear Dude:

I'm in a major bind. I have just relocated to Chicago and have no idea where to score quality bud and the associated paraphernalia — bongs, pipes, one-hitters, papers, etc. It's a huge bummer. I know you know Chicago.

Hook me up, dude.

Dear Bro:

Good news. Bad news. First the bad. Unlike tropical tourist destinations, you're not going to score a bag of dirt weed at dirt-cheap prices. This ain't Jamaica, bro. This is Chicago. This is America. Now the good news. A little common sense will help with your bud-quest. Two groups you should get cozy with: college students and artists. While more and more people are smoking these days — 70 million Americans have at least tried reefer once — your best bet is to hang in areas frequented by the aforementioned demographic. Lurk around and make friends in the coffee shops, the bars, and the record stores in the following neighborhoods.

In **Wicker Park/Bucktown** (roughly bounded by Western Avenue, Fullerton Avenue, the Kennedy Expressway, and Division Street), the **Flat Iron Building** (1579 North Milwaukee Avenue) is a hangout for freaks, geeks, and geniuses. This massive, triangular, three-story building plays home and studio to a cornucopia of artists, anarchists, punkers, goths, poets, writers, party animals, people who need to take a bath, tattoo artists, puppet makers, body piercers, and total weirdoes. Walk the halls of this building and you'll discover all sorts of cool galleries, art studios, and loft apartments. It's the perfect place to score some herb if you can hook up with the right people. Remember, make some friends, but don't be too over-the-top or pushy, bro. You don't want to be mistaken for a narc.

Next 'hood on your smoke quest should definitely be **Pilsen** (bounded by 16th Street, Halsted Street, the Chicago River, and Damen Avenue). This neighborhood was initially settled by Czechs, but around 1950 it started transforming into a Mexican enclave. If you get the munchies, bro, you'll find some absolutely killer enchiladas (see "Secret Mexican"). In the last decade or so, artists and college students have flocked to this area because of its close proximity to downtown and affordable loft spaces. Wander down Halsted, where bohemian coffee shops and artists' studios are centralized. You might find a hook-up here.

As for your search for paraphernalia, look around the Clark and Belmont area. Definitely pay a visit to **Egor's Dungeon** (900 West Belmont Avenue, 773-525-7131), a small shop predominantly dedicated to selling bondage ware and the associated accessories (ball gags, whips, cuffs, etc.). Inquire at the counter about smoke-related goods and the clerk will produce a catalog of weed-related items. The store stocks most everything from the catalog — it's just kept discreetly hidden in the back. Around the corner, the **Alley** (858 West Belmont Avenue, 773-883-1800) has a decent selection of pipes kept in a glass case in the lower level of the store. The Alley is a part of the **Alternative Shopping Complex**, which is really just a slew of stores geared toward disenchanted suburban pseudo punks. This is a crazy place, bro. These shops sell everything from overpriced candles to overpriced clothing to overpriced incense to overpriced plaster columns . . . well, you get the point.

For a head shop that's a little more bohemian — more, no pun intended, grassroots — try **Adam's Apple** (6229 North California Avenue, 773-338-4567). The store is very small and low key, and it's been around since the '60s.

SECRET
HIGH TEA

It's one of life's more refined, more dignified pleasures. Afternoon tea. Think about it — what better way to escape winter's biting wind than by sipping a cup of hot tea?

High tea, fountain side, at the **Palm Court** at the **Drake Hotel** (140 East Walton Street, 312-787-2200) is a delight. The Drake, built in 1920, is one of Chicago's classic and classiest hotels. The décor is opulent and reminiscent of an old-world Renaissance palace. Over the years, the hotel has hosted notable guests from Pope John Paul II to Walt Disney. Each afternoon in the spacious Palm Court, a harpist plays softly in the background as patrons sip tea.

A favorite spot for mothers and daughters to visit is **American Girl Cafe** (111 East Chicago Avenue, 312-943-9400), located inside the gargantuan **American Girl Place** store. The entire complex is devoted to the expensive line of American Girl dolls, books, clothing, accessories, and magazines. Every doll comes with its own story, a background, and history. It's a spectacle but young girls adore it. On the second floor is the café, where lines of kids and parents can get thick in the afternoons. The café is a strange affair to the uninitiated, as it's decorated in pink-and-black polka dots and stripes, lit a little too brightly, and has tables equipped with high chairs for all the little girls' dolls. Tea service runs from 2:30 PM to 4 PM.

One last place for tea, away from all the downtown hubbub, is **Villa Kula** (4518 North Lincoln Avenue, 773-728-3114), which offers 17 different blends of black, green, and white teas, as well as an assortment of herbal infusions called tisanes. This cozy storefront restaurant, nestled in the old-world German neighborhood of Lincoln Square, offers four different menus throughout the day.

SECRET
HOITY-TOITY

Much of this book focuses on greasy spoons, red-and-white-checkered tablecloths, and super-cheap menus. At least to this writer, these places are the real "Secret Chicago." But now it's time to go upscale. So pick up that suit or dress at the dry cleaners, shower up, and head out for a glitzy evening of wining and dining. Better bring your platinum credit card and make sure you're not over the limit. You can blow a lot of money at these places and washing dishes ain't an option.

Chicago's uber-celebrity chef is Charlie Trotter, the best-selling author of countless cookbooks and a staple of the late-night talk show circuit. How this man became the god of the Chi-town kitchen is beyond me. He couldn't grill an Italian sausage the Chicago way if his culinary license depended on it (he'd have to poach it, smother it with a bordelaise sauce, and side it with ratatouille). To me, Charlie Trotter is more suited to the glitz and glam of LA, where the Wolfgang Pucks and the Spagos of the world abound. But many Chicagoans obviously disagree. **Charlie Trotter's** (816 West Armitage Avenue, 773-248-6228) is a renowned gourmet restaurant, receiving rave reviews from food critics and customers the world over. It's worth trying, at least to see what all the hoopla is about. But prepare yourself for sticker shock — this dining experience will cost you. As a friend of mine put it, "I don't have enough money to piss in that restaurant!" Still, there is good reason for all the fuss. The restaurant is in an ivy-blanketed brick brownstone in Chicago's tony Lincoln Park neighborhood. *Les repas*, of the freshest organic ingredients, are prepared under Trotter's hawk eye (he's a notorious culinary fascist).

The food is spectacular, and the international menu changes constantly, so go ahead, spend a month's salary.

Another pricey but worthy restaurant where all the pretty power people come out to play is **One Sixtyblue** (160 North Loomis Street, 312-850-0303). It has long been rumored that Michael Jordan is a silent partner in this trendy hot spot, named for its address and the color of the exterior (don't ask, I think it's silly too). The décor, created by restaurant designer Adam Tihany, is urban chic — meaning lots of glass and steel cables. And the cuisine is sophisticated contemporary. Another regular stop for the haute couture trendoids is **Blackbird** (619 West Randolph Street, 312-715-0708). Chef Paul Kahan has created an inventive contemporary American menu that changes seasonally. If it's available, order the Asian pear and Hudson Valley Camembert tart.

SECRET
HOT DOGS

If you were to narrow it down — I mean, really narrow it down — Chicago would be known for pizza and the blues, architecture and Michael Jordan, Al Capone and hot dogs. You could toss in a few others, but hot dogs would definitely be right in the mix. Why? According to weenie-lore, Chicago is where it all started. In 1893, two young immigrants from Austria-Hungary toted their secret frankfurter recipe to World's Columbian Exposition in Chicago. The secret was burying the juicy frank in a toasted golden-brown bun and piling it high with yellow mustard, green relish, diced onion, sliced tomato, sport peppers, a kosher pickle spear, and a sprinkling of celery salt. History was made. The sandwich quickly earned the moniker "the Chicago-style hot dog." Today, the Vienna all-beef hot dog recipe is served up by 2,000 vendors across the city — from far north to far south, from the lakeshore all the way west to the edge of the suburbs. There's no mistaking the Vienna logo: a hot dog placed over a bold blue *V*. You'll see it no matter where you are in Chicago. In fact, there are more Vienna Beef hot dog vendors in the city than there are Burger King, Wendy's, and McDonald's outlets combined. The **Vienna Sausage Manufacturing Company** (2501 North Damen Avenue, 773-278-7800), on the city's North Side, pumps out 15 million hot dogs a year. But what many people don't realize is that the company has a hot dog stand within the factory itself, open to the public, serving up the freshest hot dogs you'll ever bite into. The best measure of how good these red hots are is the crowd inside the **Vienna Factory Store**. The majority of the patrons are Vienna factory workers, still wearing white lab jackets and hairnets and sitting down for dogs loaded with the works.

Venturing away from the Vienna Factory Store, you'll discover a shop underneath the elevated train tracks that makes a mean dog. **Demon Dogs** (944 West Fullerton Avenue, 773-281-2001) sits under the rumbling train stop at the Fullerton Avenue station, which makes it convenient for those days you're on your way home and don't want to cook. It has a cool collection of rock 'n' roll memorabilia from bands that have stopped by and fallen in love with the mouth-watering red hots. Another popular weenie haven with the locals is the **Weiner's Circle** (2622 North Clark Street, 773-477-7444). Many consider the dogs here to be the best in the city. Another plus: it's open until 4 AM. Another Chi-town hot dog institution is **Byron's Hot Dog Haus**, with three locations (1017 West Irving Park Road, 773-281-7474;

680 North Halsted Street, 312-266-3355; and 1701 West Lawrence Avenue, 773-271-0900). Just 20 minutes west of downtown, in suburban Forest Park, **Parky's** (329 South Harlem Avenue, Forest Park, 708-366-3090) is a neighborhood institution. This little A-frame restaurant has weenies to die for. Finally, the quest for a great hot dog just wouldn't be complete without a stop at **Superdawg** (6363 North Milwaukee Avenue, 773-763-0660). A throwback to a bygone era, Superdawg has carhops who deliver your food — delicious dogs — on a window tray. Plus, the giant Mr. and Mrs. Hot Dog on top of this 1948 landmark are worth a look-see with or without the chow. Bob's Big Boy, eat your heart out.

S E C R E T
ICE CREAM

For over 75 years, **Petersen's** (1104 West Chicago Avenue, Oak Park, 708-386-6131) has scooped up gooey ice cream that's heavy on the real cream. It offers around 20 flavors, including a great eggnog ice cream around the holidays. The root beer float is stupendous, frothing over with suds and vanilla. When my mom was a kid, this is where she went on summer nights.

Swiss Gourmet Ice Cream Parlor (2187 North Clybourn Avenue, 773-755-4616), right across the street from the popular Webster Place cinema, serves rich and tasty ice cream and is the perfect stop after a show. Owner Marty Cain grew up in the dairy business and, for over 50 years, his family has operated Brown Dairy out of Valparaiso, Indiana. It's this long tradition that shows in the excellent ice cream, the fine service, and the old-fashioned parlor charm of this store.

Over the course of a year, the shop rotates nearly 100 flavors. Some of the favorites include Peppermint Stick and Dee-licious Fresh Peach.

Zephyr Ice Cream Restaurant (1777 West Wilson Avenue, 773-728-6070) is the ideal spot to bring a date late on a Friday night. The setting puts a spin on the traditionally bright parlor motif, adding Art Deco booths and mirrored walls. The ice cream is super rich and thick, perfect for those who fear no fat.

When I was a kid, we took a family trip to San Francisco. My favorite memory? Ghirardelli Square and all that fabulous chocolate. There are only a few **Ghirardelli Chocolate Shop & Soda Fountains** east of San Francisco Bay and Chicago claims one (830 North Michigan Avenue, 312-337-9330). And you know what? The sweets are every bit as good as I remember. With old-fashioned, marble-topped tables and an antique-looking soda fountain, the challenge at this place is what not to eat. The shop is filled with all sorts of milk, dark, and semi-sweet chocolates, coffees, and ice creams. But the item to make your child's eyes widen (or yours) is the Earthquake Sundae — a family-sized concoction that serves at least four. What is it? Try eight flavors of ice cream, eight toppings, bananas, and whipped cream, all piled high and punctuated with nuts and cherries.

SECRET
ICE SKATING

Go ahead. Embrace it — winter in Chicago. Don't just live with it, love it. It's going to be here for a while — so celebrate inclement weather, extol its intemperate, volatile virtue, and give Old Man Winter a big bear hug. Dig out that old wool ski sweater and those thick, itchy wool socks. Act like a kid again. Wear a stocking cap with a floppy yarn ball on the end. Wear mittens instead of gloves. Call a friend and go ice skating.

Spend a perfect, chilly winter day at the ice skating rink at **Daley Bicentennial Plaza** (337 East Randolph Street, 312-742-7648). Nestled into a hilly alcove on the north end of Grant Park, this rink is the first in the city to open and, each spring, the last to close. Weather permitting, skating season opens on the last Saturday in November. Not far away, the rink atop **Navy Pier** (600 East Grand Avenue, 312-595-7437) affords skaters a stunning view of Chicago's skyline. But be careful and dress warmly — because Navy Pier is right on Lake Michigan, the wind can be a snapping, whipping, cold jolt to the senses. But that's part of the fun, right?

On the South Side, the rink at **Midway Plaisance Park** (East 59th Street to East 60th Street and South Stony Island to South Cottage Grove, 312-747-7661) is a better-kept secret than the downtown ice skating venues. It's also a beautiful setting for a day on the ice. The rink is just one part of the 80-acre median that runs from Jackson Park to Washington Park through the University of Chicago. The expanse was designed by Frederick Law Olmsted for the 1893 World's Columbian Exposition and, during the fair, played host to the first-ever Ferris wheel. The origin of the carnival term "midway" derives from this park and the 1893 exposition.

However, if you want to escape the bite of Chicago's winter, pay a visit to **McFetridge Sports Center** (3843 North California Avenue, 312-742-7585). This Olympic-sized rink, open year round, is indoors and offers skating instructions and hockey leagues.

For something even more off the beaten path, you might want to call several of the Chicago Park District's community parks that, weather permitting, create ice ponds. These parks are more remote and less crowded. But, please, call first to make sure that there is ice to skate on.

On the South Side, **Ogden Park** (6500 South Racine Avenue, 312-747-6572) is a roomy 60-acre space perfect for family outings all year long. Cross-country skiers often frequent this natural sanctuary. On the West Side is **Douglas Park** (1401 South Sacramento Avenue, 312-747-7460), a 174-acre expanse. When the weather outside is frightful, the park sets up a good old-fashioned ice pond.

S E C R E T
INDIAN
✤

If you love Indian food as I do, you cannot go wrong by trekking up to Devon Avenue in the city's far North Side. Chicago's Indian community is centered here in the West Ridge neighborhood. If you stroll a few blocks in either direction on Devon and close your eyes, you will be blanketed in the warm aromas of Indian cuisine. **Sher-A-Punjab** (2510 West Devon Avenue, 773-973-4000), with its spread-out buffet, is dangerous. The food is so good and there's so much of it, you may need a stretcher when it's time to leave. For $8, you get an all-you-can-eat meal of vegetarian, chicken, and lamb dishes bathed in spicy sauces, piping hot naan bread, and platters of delectable chicken and lamb tandoori. **Udupi Palace** (2543 West Devon Avenue, 773-338-2152) is a winner for the vegetarian crowd — there's no meat to be found anywhere on the menu. The food is South Indian, meaning lots of rice-and-lentil-based entrées, spiced with red pepper and coriander. **Moti Mahal** (1031 West Belmont Avenue, 773-472-0095;

2525 West Devon Avenue, 773-262-2080) is one of those places that
locals suggest to one another. It's a hole-in-the-wall establishment,
with just a few tables and a bring-your-own-booze policy. The naan
is delicious, light, and steaming hot. Hell, everything here is good.

SECRET
ITALIAN ICE

Summer nights outside **Mario's Italian Lemonade** (1066 West
Taylor Street) are quintessentially Chicago. Mario's is a one-story red
and white wooden shack in the heart of the Little Italy neighborhood, and it's open each year from May to September. Above the
shack, cheapie plastic patio lights are lit up like multicolored fireflies
after the high summer sun has vanished somewhere out over the
western suburbs. After dinner, a crowd emerges on Little Italy's main
drag — Taylor Street. The swarm is a melting pot of students from
the nearby University of Illinois at Chicago, old-time Italians, and
city folk — black, white, Latino, Asian — from every corner of town
who have made the trek to Taylor. Humid nights are the best time to
visit, when the air is heavy and your T-shirt sticks to your skin. A cup
of Mario's refreshing Italian ice cools your hot mouth — it's an overwhelming blast of shaved ice mixed with tiny bits of fresh fruit and
sweet juice. In all, there are 16 flavors, including cantaloupe, lemon,
watermelon, cherry, and grape. There was a time in Chicago when
Italian ice stands and carts were not an anomaly like this one is. They
stood on many street corners in most neighborhoods. Today, they
have all but vanished like that summer sun, leaving Mario's as one of
the last hopes for a sweet summer chill.

SECRET JAZZ

In the 1920s, jazz musicians journeyed to Chicago from the South as word of the Windy City's happening club and recording studio scene spread like wildfire. Live jazz broadcasts crackled from the megawatt Chicago radio stations. Clubs hopped and bopped well past the blue hour. Many jazz greats honed their chops in Chi-town. Think Louis Armstrong, Sidney Bechet, Bix Beiderbecke, Benny Goodman, Gene Krupa, and Jelly Roll Morton. The list goes on until sunrise. Present-day Chicago jazz is as smooth and swanky as ever, with a grand old history and a bright new future. First stop on your finger-snappin' tour should be the **Green Mill** (4802 North Broadway Street, 773-878-5552). This venerable jazz institution opened in 1907 and the music has never stopped. It is the oldest continuously operating jazz club in the country. Al Capone frequented the Mill (mob hits went down here). Charlie Chaplin even favored the Mill for late-afternoon libations. If you stop in, ask the bartender for the scrapbook. A tattered three-ring binder holds all the newspaper clippings from over the years that have mentioned this watering hole and music venue. From the flickering green neon above the entrance to the dark wood paneling to the high-octane cocktails, this place is as good as it gets. For nightly lineups, consult a *Chicago Reader* or a *New City* (see "Secret Periodicals").

The **Jazz Showcase** (59 West Grand Avenue, 312-670-2473) is the première jazz venue for aficionados. For over 50 years, this great club has been a place that people swarm to hear the music. This isn't a place to schmooze. Smoking ain't allowed. This isn't a place to pick up chicks. This isn't a place for trendoids looking to emulate Dean

Martin. This is a place to — get this — down a beer and listen to the best jazz in Chicago. Acoustic jazz at that. No trippy fusion or electrified acid-jazz meanderings here. If you are looking for something a little bit more upscale, however, **Pops for Champagne** (2934 North Sheffield Avenue, 773-472-1000) is a great place to impress a date. Ritzy. Intimate. Expensive as hell. This is where the chic clientele come after hours to blow $388 on a bottle of Cristal Vintage Rosé. The bands play on a tiny little stage behind the bar. The acoustics are wonderful, and the setting highly romantic. Too bad the service is so damned pretentious. If you're more interested in jazz with a gritty, urban pulse, check out the **Velvet Lounge** (2128-1/2 South Indiana Avenue, 312-791-9050). While the neighborhood around this classic club is gentrifying fast, it's still a bit on the seamy side. Not far away, the **Cotton Club** (1710 South Michigan Avenue, 312-341-9787) is an upscale jazz joint named after the famous club in Harlem, New York. There are two rooms for tunes here: the smaller, low-key Cab Calloway room and the gray room, offering up great sounds. This is a favorite spot with the well-to-do African-American crowd. **Green Dolphin Street** (2200 North Ashland Avenue, 773-395-0066) is an elegant jazz supper club with a fine dining room, a dark cozy bar, and a lounge that showcases traditional jazz, as well as big band. It also has a humidor filled with fine stogies. One more fine stop for serious jazz enthusiasts is **Andy's** (11 East Hubbard Street, 312-642-6805). The coolest thing about this place is that, because it caters to the downtown working crowd, it has a free noontime jazz set Monday through Friday.

Another really hip venue, just loaded with cool nouveaux-urban ambience, is the **HotHouse** (31 East Balbo Avenue, 312-362-9707). With vast windows looking out on the old and weathered South Loop district, this progressive arts center schedules an eclectic mix of avant-garde jazz, as well as world music and cabaret acts. You'll also find poetry readings, paintings, sculpture, and performance art on the monthly slate. Extremely cool.

If you've been combing record stores for that long out-of-print jazz obscurity, try the **Jazz Record Mart** (444 North Wabash Avenue, 312-222-1467). This is the largest jazz specialty store in the whole wide world. With more than 20,000 CDs and 30,000 vinyl albums, if you don't find it here, just give up already. Owner Bob Koester, the founder of the Delmark Records label, also lines up an impressive bevy of in-store appearances by local and national jazz faves.

And before we forget, there's the **Chicago Jazz Festival** held every Labor Day weekend in Grant Park (312-744-3315, bounded by the lakeshore, Randolph Street, Roosevelt Road, and Michigan Avenue). While it can't compete with the Festival International de Jazz de Montréal or the long-running Monterey Jazz Fest in California, it is the largest free outdoor jazz fest in the world.

SECRET

JEWELRY

✿

Jeweler's Row is where I bought my wife's engagement ring. It's a two-block strip along Wabash Avenue between Washington Boulevard and Monroe Street. Crammed into this confining urban space are countless jewelry stores with street-side window displays brimming with sparkling gems. It really does twinkle here, even on the grayest winter day and under the shadow of the elevated tracks above Wabash. Of course, some of the sparkle comes from strategically set high-powered spotlights hitting the gems at just the right angles. But the real reason why Wabash glimmers is that this is one of the largest wholesale jewelry districts in the country. At the risk of sounding like a cheesy radio ad, if you're in the market for a diamond, this is where you want to go. You can walk into one shop, price a diamond, and then comparison shop at the other stores in one outing. The savings here are huge. Many of these shops are suppliers to mall jewelry stores around the country. The **Jeweler's Center,** at the **Mallers Building** (5 South Wabash Avenue), is an old high-rise full of jewelers hawking gold watches, costume jewelry, semiprecious stones, sterling silver rings, and other such baubles. Wander inside and climb your way up. You can find loose-stone dealers, custom designers, engravers, gold dealers, platinum dealers, watch dealers, pearl importers, and jewelry appraisers here. I bought a loose diamond at a store that had the best price, then had a platinum band designed in a small designer's office upstairs. The diamond dealer set the stone and I saved quite a bit. It's a good deal and it's actually kind of a fun process. And if you're interested, the dealer that gave me the great price was **State & Company** (9 North Wabash Avenue, 312-795-9200 or 1-800-765-3989).

SECRET
JUKEBOXES
❧

One of the virtues of any good watering hole is good music. And that music should reflect the tavern itself: its people and its atmosphere. Sometimes, when you're on the precipice of that perfect booze buzz, a classic song in the background can send you into that besotted state of euphoria. Jukeboxes don't have the importance in our society that they once had. That's too bad. But here are a few choice taverns where they still matter a whole lot.

Delilah's (2771 North Lincoln Avenue, 773-472-2771), in my opinion, has the best jukebox in the city. Of course, jukebox preference depends entirely on your musical tastes. Delilah's is a dark, punky, two-story rock club. The beer selection is vast and the patrons are of the body-pierced/tattoo crowd. The jukebox selection is like going to a friend's house and salivating over his music collection. From Johnny Cash to the Sex Pistols to Hank Williams to Social Distortion. Eclectic and very cool.

Song worth your dollar: "Folsom Prison Blues" by Johnny Cash.

Old Town Ale House (219 West North Avenue, 312-944-7020) is an oddity in one of Chicago's ritziest neighborhoods. The crowd is a bedraggled lot of burned-out writers, hoarse-throated theater actors, and soul-searching art students. The shabby bar doesn't look like it's had a spring cleaning since it opened in 1958. Bookshelves are lined with classics like Twain and Shakespeare, and stacks of reference books to prove wrong that opinionated asshole sitting next to you. But the best thing about this place is the jukebox, packed with a keen mix of torch singers and jazz trios, classical overtures and Motown classics. Where else will you find Dizzy Gillespie and the Beatles sharing the same bill?

Song worth your buck: "Willow Weep for Me" by Billie Holiday.

Schuba's (3159 North Southport Avenue, 773-525-2508) has a great docket of live rock, alternative country, folk, and rockabilly bands throughout the week. But that's in the back room of the club, where you'll find the main stage. In the front room, by the bar, you'll discover the best selection of indie pop and local Chicago artists in any jukebox in the city. There's also a nice mix of Americana and alt.country tunes.

Song worth your single: "Faker" by Diane Izzo.

Holiday Club (1471 North Milwaukee Avenue, 773-486-0686) is a hangout for hardcore swingers — and I don't mean people who trade spouses. This is a Rat Pack–style bar, complete with a back room called the Bamboo Lounge where you'll hear swanky Vegas lounge grooves and sip on coconut-shell cocktails. If you're into the retro fad, you need look no further. But the jukebox isn't restricted to Dean, Frank, and Sammy. Slide a buck in the slot and you'll hear the kind of musical fusion that gives a corporate radio program director nightmares. Earth, Wind and Fire, Naked Ray Gun, Tony Bennett. Who needs radio?

Song worth your greenback: "My Kinda Town" by Frank Sinatra.

S E C R E T
KIDS

I was eight years old the first time I saw Chicago. We came in from the west on the Eisenhower Expressway, and the skyline just grew and grew until it filled the windshield of the family car, a sky-blue Chevy Suburban. My mom grew up in Chicago. My dad had spent years there, too. But they were as wide-eyed as my two older sisters, my older brother, and I, sitting in the back of the car with this enormous metropolis of steel and shiny glass suddenly engulfing us on every side. To a child, Chicago may as well be the Emerald City of Oz, rising from out of nowhere, magical and full of life. We craned our necks near the windows of the car to spot the tops of all the huge buildings. We passed the Art Institute, where children climbed up on the lion statues out front. Families stood along Michigan Avenue posing for pictures, flashbulbs popping. Along the lakefront, colorful kites were sent aloft. Sunbathers stretched on the silky sand of Oak Street Beach. Waves lapped gently on the shore. Everywhere: energy and excitement. I was amazed. Nearly 27 years later, I am still enthralled.

There is a lot to do in the city if you're young and full of life and energy. First things first: you want to see the city from the highest vantage point possible. The **Sears Tower** (233 South Wacker Drive, 312-875-9696) is the tallest building in the United States and the second tallest in the world. Only the Petronas Towers in Malaysia climb higher into the sky, and they cheated by adding spires to give the buildings a leg up on the tallest-building-in-the-world competition. Still, the Sears Tower is terrific. Take the super-fast one-minute elevator ride up 1,355 feet to the 103rd floor, where you'll find the Skydeck. On a crystal-clear day, you can see 60 miles in every direction. That means you can spy Wisconsin, Indiana, and even Michigan, all the way across the lake.

Next stop is **Navy Pier** and the **Chicago Children's Museum** (700 East Grand Avenue, 312-527-1000). This 57,000-square-foot museum is one massive playground. There's an indoor nature trail, a PlayMaze, an inventing lab, and interactive musical performances. What makes this place really special is the emphasis on imagination and creativity, a fresh idea in an age of violent video games marketed toward children. An all-day pass is $6; infants under one year get in free. Thursday evenings, from 5 PM to 8 PM, are free family nights.

For lunch, take the kids to any number of loud theme restaurants. Many are huddled in one pocket of downtown called River North.

Buyer beware — you can drop a sizeable chunk of your weekly salary at these joints, but kids love them. **Ed Debevic's** (640 North Wells Street, 312-664-1707) is an interactive, '50s-style diner with waiters whose shtick is to cop an attitude. Every so often the whole wait staff drops what it's doing, climbs up on a countertop, and belts out a doo-wop song or two. Other popular theme establishments are the **Rainforest Cafe** (605 North Clark Street, 312-787-1501) and the **Rock & Roll McDonald's** (600 North Clark Street, 312-664-7940), which is decked out with old jukeboxes and rock memorabilia.

What would a day out with the family be without a trip to the zoo? The **Lincoln Park Zoo** (2200 North Cannon Drive, 312-742-2000) operates a kid-pleaser petting farm, and it's free. The **Brookfield Zoo** (8400 West 31st Street, Brookfield, 708-485-0263) spotlights a tropical rain forest where apes walk about freely. Another popular nature habitat is the **John G. Shedd Aquarium** (1200 South Lake Shore Drive, 312-939-2438), notable for its oceanarium, housing beluga whales, dolphins, and sea otters. The 90,000-gallon coral reef exhibit is a habitat for 8,000 creatures. At 11 AM and 2 PM, divers take to the tanks and hand feed the aquatic animals. But beware: in summer, the crowds are so thick that your child may not have a chance to see the feeding unless you kick/shove your way to the glass. It is not a pretty scene. Better to go early in the morning and leave when the masses file in around noon, or to arrive late in the afternoon, when the lines dissipate and you can actually see some of the tanks.

Ever since I was a kid, I've loved dinosaurs. Somewhere in an old cardboard box is an 8mm home movie of me, at six, excavating for dinosaur bones in my backyard. What child doesn't marvel at these prehistoric creatures? The best collection of dino bones in Chicago is at the **Field Museum of Natural History** (Lake Shore Drive and East Roosevelt Road, 312-922-9410). In the lobby is Sue, the largest complete T-Rex dinosaur fossil ever discovered. You can find out more about this great museum, which has a collection of more than 20,000 artifacts, at www.fmnh.org.

I am a die-hard Cubs fan, but I must admit that **Comiskey Park** (333 West 35th Street, 312-674-1000), where the White Sox play, caters to the family crowd more than **Wrigley Field** (1060 West Addison Street, 773-404-2827) does. Comiskey has lots of between-inning shenanigans, songs, contests, music, and even an exploding scoreboard that shoots off fireworks when a home-team hitter belts a home run. Saturdays, after the game, there's a marvelous fireworks display over the park.

Can't get to Disneyland? Or Great America, for that matter? You need not venture much further than downtown. **DisneyQuest** (55 East Ohio Street, 312-222-1300) has five stories of interactive (read: hyperactive) computer games and pulse-pounding virtual reality rides. Take a ride (and get wet) on a virtual cyber-coaster on CyberSpace Mountain or plunge down raging rapids in the virtual Jungle Cruise.

Why not forsake all the hyper attractions and take your kids to a good old-fashioned puppet show? The **Puppet Parlor** (1922 West Montrose Avenue, 773-2919) is home to the National Marionette Company, which performs original stories and classic fairy-tale adaptations.

When I was a kid, I loved freight trains. Come to think of it, I still do. While some people moan and groan when forced to wait at a train traffic signal, I get excited counting all the cars gathered from all corners of the country. I also love the lonely bellow of a train's whistle in the night. So, of course, I think model trains are pretty cool. If you don't have the time or money to build your own set, the **Museum of Science and Industry** (5700 South Lake Shore Drive,

773-684-1414) has a huge setup with working trains, signals, lights, and whistles — 1,200 feet of track in all, spread over a beautiful 3,000-square-foot display. You can stand for a long nostalgic time just staring. And while you're here, you may as well explore the entire museum. Sure, it's a tourist trap — after all, it's the busiest attraction in the entire Midwest — but with 14 acres of interactive displays, an authentic World War II submarine, and an Omnimax theatre, it's worth wading through the crowd. You can learn more about the MSI at www.msichicago.org.

And here's something only a handful of locals know about: every Tuesday around 6 PM, young uber-geniuses convene at the **Rudy Lozano Branch Public Library** (1805 South Loomis Street, 312-746-4329) to play in the **Knight Moves Chess Club**. Head librarian Hector Hernandez, a state-ranked chess player, gives lessons to kids of all ages. One of Hernandez's pupils recently reached the rank of number 24 in the country for his age group. But you need not be an expert player to partake in the fun. Many families come out with little to no knowledge of the game of chess. And best of all, it's free.

SECRET
KISSING

Here are just a few of my top choices for places to make a romantic memory. From late spring to early autumn, **Buckingham Fountain** (Grant Park, at Lake Shore Drive and Congress Parkway) is simply splendid. This 1927 monument in Georgia pink marble, fashioned from the fountains of Versailles, has regular light and water shows each evening. With Lake Michigan to the east and the skyline to the west, there's no better place to steal a kiss. Just a short walk south, along the edge of the Shedd Aquarium, is a majestic view of the city. Another picturesque spot for a little *amour* is the America Windows within the **Art Institute of Chicago** (Michigan Avenue and Adams Street, 312-443-3600). This masterpiece of midnight-blue stained glass by artist Marc Chagall inspires spontaneous romance. Hey, it was good enough for Ferris Bueller. If you're looking for a little solitude, try Lincoln Park, across from Addison Avenue. Walk through the woods toward Lake Michigan and head south along the lakeshore until you reach the rocky peninsula of **Belmont Harbor**. From here, you get a beautiful view of the city from the north. You can scale the concrete steps and sit right at the water's edge. In winter, the surrounding park is perfect for a snowball fight and a romantic roll in the snow. If you're shooting for sophistication, the **Signature Lounge at the 96th** (875 North Michigan Avenue, 312-787-9596), high atop the John Hancock Center, provides a twinkling, kiss-perfect nocturnal view of downtown Chicago. Wait patiently for one of the super-desirable window-side tables, and bring lots of dough. Everything in here is expensive. They even charge for the peanuts on the table.

SECRET
KITES
❦

Kite flying is coming back with muscle. The best place to, excuse the expression, "go fly a kite," is **Cricket Hill** at **Montrose Beach** (Montrose Avenue and the lakeshore). Here, you will find dozens of high-flying enthusiasts lofting their kites into the skies. Bob Zavell, owner of **Kite Harbor** (109 Marion Street, Oak Park, 708-848-4907), says the best time to fly a kite is spring or fall, because of the wind. But Zavell adds that, with new technology, you can fly a kite with virtually no wind at all. Kite Harbor carries several stunt kites that can fly no matter what the conditions. Other standout areas for lofting a kite are **North Avenue Beach** (North Avenue and the lakeshore) and **Grant Park** (bounded by the lakefront, Randolph Street, Roosevelt Road, and Michigan Avenue).

SECRET
KITSCH
❦

Things really do go in cycles. Case in point — Afros and platform shoes, polyester shirts and bell bottoms. In the '70s, they were cool. Then . . . they weren't. Go figure, they're cool again. And all this retro madness certainly isn't relegated to just the "Have a Nice Day" decade. Don't ask me why, but the '80s are now coming into play. Just a few years ago, hipsters were cackling at synth-rockers like Duran Duran, but now they're extolling their virtues. It won't be long before you see someone in parachute pants, trust me. Chicago has many places to satiate your craving for kitsch. Start at **Strange Cargo** (3448 North Clark Street, 773-327-8090), a shop stuffed to the rafters with pop-culture curios. You'll find vintage posters of John Travolta circa *Saturday Night Fever*, glossy 8-by-10 photos of former teen heartthrob Leif Garrett, and new T-shirts emblazoned with a "Charlie's Angels" or "Dukes of Hazzard" logo. It also sells stickers and trading cards from the '70s, unopened and in the original packaging.

It's groovy, baby. At **Right-on Futon** (1184 North Milwaukee Avenue, 773-235-2533; 3012 North Lincoln Avenue, 773-528-3960), they take their kitsch very seriously. They stock more than 20 colors of lava lamps, as well as piles and piles of multi-colored beanbags. Not only do they sell tons of futon pads and frames, but they also custom build really hip '50s-style dinette tables and chairs in every shade. One popular barstool design has an eerie glow-in-the dark eyeball on the cushion. For more info on this duo of really cool and crafty stores, navigate to their Web site at www.rightonfuton.com. And if that isn't enough kitsch, you can dine at **Kitsch'n on Roscoe** (2005 West Roscoe Street, 773-248-7372) and feel like a Brady. From the bright Formica kitchen tables to the Crayola-hued linoleum floor, the only thing missing is Alice and Tiger. Selections on the menu include green eggs and ham with spinach pesto and a super-sweet Pop-Tart sundae. With groovy '70s tunes playing in the background, this is a kitsch-lover's delight. By the way — I still have a crush on Marcia Brady. Marcia, Marcia, Marcia.

SECRET
LAKE SHORE DRIVE

Here's a little-known fact about Chicago's magnificent Lake Shore Drive that I learned the hard way. Traffic ordinance 0-072-020 prohibits the use of commercial vehicles on boulevards in Chicago. This means no pickup trucks or vans or recreational vehicles with business license plates. Years ago, I owned a pickup truck with commercial plates. Well, even though Chicago's finest say you can't drive a vehicle of this nature on Lake Shore Drive, this stupid law is not posted anywhere in the city. No signs. No nothing. Still, I was slapped with a $50 fine. The moral of this story: stay off LSD if you have a larger-sized vehicle with business tags.

SECRET
LAND OF OZ

L. Frank Baum, the fanciful author behind *The Wonderful Wizard of Oz*, as well as many other imaginative books in the Oz series, lived in Chicago between 1891 and 1908. During his tenure as a Windy City resident, Baum earned national notoriety with the success of his children's books *Mother Goose in Prose* and *Father Goose, His Book*. *Father Goose* sold an impressive 75,000 copies in its first year of release and was cited in the *Tribune* as the best-selling children's book of 1899. A year later, Baum was skipping down the yellow brick road with *The Wonderful Wizard of Oz*. Baum and *Wizard of Oz* illustrator William W. Denslow collaborated on the book in 1900 in a 10th-floor studio within the **Fine Arts Building** (410 South Michigan Avenue). For more on this grand old building, check out "Secret Architecture." Much of the book, however, was conceptualized in Baum's North Side home at 1667 North Humboldt Boulevard, where a seven-foot marker of distinction was placed in 1997 to commemorate the site. Each year at the end of July, the city of Chicago sponsors the **Oz Festival** (2200 North Cannon Drive, 773-409-5466), a popular party in Lincoln Park that includes music, food, and crafts along with floating art on the Lincoln Park Lagoon. Not surprisingly, the theme of this colorful and energetic fest is *The Wonderful Wizard of Oz*. And finally, if you are a fan of the Oz stories, you may want to visit **Oz**

Park (2021 North Burling Street, 312-742-7898). Standing over the park entrance is a shiny statue of Baum's character the Tin Man, while at the southeast end is a statue of the Cowardly Lion. The park has a small playground for kids and is a favorite stomp, romp, and roll area for local dogs.

S E C R E T

LAWN ART

Certain homeowners are hell-bent on doing something with their front yards other than erecting the typical flower-bearing wheelbarrow or wooden house bird feeder. Lawn art isn't for everyone, but it makes for interesting conversation. The **House of Crosses** (1544 West Chestnut Street) is one man's front-yard paean to stars of the silver screen. This two-story frame house is peppered with hundreds of wooden crosses, reflective stickers, shields, and plaques that pay tribute to cinema icons like Bing Crosby, Tyrone Power, Zsa Zsa Gabor, and Doris Day among many, many others. This place is a real head-scratcher. But my favorite display of lawn-art eccentricity in Chicago is just a foul ball away from Wrigley Field at **1110 Addison Street**. On your way to a Cubs game, stop and take a gander at the dense display of kitschy plastic Christ figures, bunny rabbits, Virgin Marys, squirrels, bearded trolls, and twirling windmills. Another attribute of this exhibition is the little metal box affixed to the wrought iron fence. Inside the box are prayer cards. If you don't need a prayer, it asks you to say one. Considering the location, how about a Cubs World Series victory? Yeah, right.

SECRET
LIBRARIES

Ever since writer A.J. Liebling called Chicago "The Second City," in a 1952 *New Yorker* issue, Chicago has had a chip on its shoulder. Some have even accused our fair city of having an inferiority complex. Sure, we like to talk in superlatives: the biggest, the baddest, the tallest, the greatest. Who doesn't? And while New York brags about the grandeur of its main public library, Chicago wins. Ha ha. The **Harold Washington Public Library** (400 South State Street, 312-747-4300) is the world's largest public library, with a collection of more than two million books. So there you have it. Inferiority complex. Hmph! The library was named for the late mayor, who was an avid reader and a driving force behind the construction of the stunning neo-Classical structure. Although not everyone is in love with the foreboding design of the building, with its gnarled rooftop gargoyles, it is impressive nonetheless. For blues fans, the library houses the Chicago blues archives. There are also films, live concerts, and author events. And the beautiful Winter Garden on the ninth floor is always worth a visit. The glass ceiling is a certain cure for anyone who suffers from light deficiency. You can pick up a monthly schedule at the library, or visit the Web site at www.chipublib.org/

Chicago's public library system includes 75 branch facilities and two larger regional libraries scattered throughout the city. Each of these locations is specifically tailored to meet the needs of the community it serves. All are open to the public — this includes locals and visitors to the city. It's a great way to fritter away the day, reading a book or a newspaper or just napping in a chair. You may run into me at the **Sulzer Regional Library** (4455 North Lincoln Avenue, 312-744-

7616). This beautiful neighborhood facility is my all-time favorite library in the city. The architecture and interior design are light, airy, and welcoming. The Sulzer employs a staff capable of speaking fluent Spanish, Korean, Chinese, French, German, Hindi, Polish, Russian, and Italian, along with using sign language to communicate with the hearing impaired. It houses a wide collection of nature materials, as well as the largest video collection of any Chicago library.

The **Newberry Library** (60 West Walton Street, 312-943-9090) is an arcane wonderland for research junkies. Among the 1.5 million bound volumes and 5.5 million manuscripts are original drawings from *Alice in Wonderland* and a leaf from the Gutenberg Bible. The collection of rare books, maps, and manuscripts is top notch. And every year at the end of July, the library hosts the **Newberry Library Book Fair** where you can feed your bibliomania by browsing over tens of thousands of donated books. Many books are cheap too — 50 cents to one dollar. Best of all, admission is free. And while you're at the fair, wander across the street from the library to the **Bughouse Square Debates**, where actors, portraying historic Chicago orators such as Clarence Darrow and Ida B. Wells, engage in spirited debates. After the re-creations, the microphones are opened for the public to address today's issues.

SECRET
LINGERIE

Want to add some spice to your sex life? Lingerie is a good start. From thigh-high boots to fishnet cat suits, you'll find all sorts of sexy unmentionables on a Chicago lingerie shopping spree.

Victoria's Secret is, by now, no secret at all. It has stores all over the US. But it does have a fine selection of tasteful unmentionables — sexy, but not so nasty as to send your lady running off and crying "pervert." Vickie's has four Chicago locations (835 North Michigan Avenue, 312-440-1169; 2628 North Clark Street, 773-549-7405; 6465 West Diversey Avenue, 773-637-2278; 7601 South Cicero Avenue, 773-582-5305), but the grand mammy is the potpourri-heavy, two-story affair on Michigan Avenue.

One recent sex fashion fetish has been the introduction of rubber, latex, and PVC lingerie into the bedroom. If this is your thing, the **House of Whacks** (3514 North Pulaski Road, 773-725-9132, fax 773-725-9137) is a reverie-filled shop for skintight and sweaty apparel for both boys and girls. It also handles lots of business by mail order or via the Web site at www.whacks.com. The Internet is an excellent way to view these sexy fashions up close and personal in full 360-degree rotation. But you'd better have your credit card handy, because this stuff ain't cheap. A latex cat suit fetches $339; a rubber French maid's dress goes for $239.

Taboo Tabou (858 West Belmont Avenue, 773-723-3739) carries all sorts of frilly lingerie, leather, and rubber wear. It also has a good selection of oils, lubes, and jellies, along with an assortment of condoms (how 'bout that glow-worm, eh?) and battery-operated adult toys. Scouring the city for something with a bit of class? Try **Isabella Fine Lingerie** (2150 North Seminary Avenue, 773-281-2352). It specializes in skimpy handmade French and Italian undies by designers like Cosabella and Donne di Piera. The tiny upscale store carries all sorts of classy chemises, teddies, and camisoles.

And lest we forget: if cross-dressing tickles your thang, **Skyscraper Heels** (2202 West Belmont Avenue, 773-477-8495, fax 773-477-8381) supplies shoes such as platforms, stilettos, and mules in sizes ranging from 5 to 15. The store also stocks elbow- and-shoulder-length leather gloves, Victorian corsets, breast forms, and nylons tailor made for the full-figured dude.

SECRET
LODGING

Breathe easy. Prices for Chicago hotel rooms are a lot gentler on the pocketbook than, say, the cost of overnighting in the Big Apple. Sure, you can max your MasterCard out if you really try, but you can also find very affordable (and comfortable) accommodations all over town.

On the high, opulent end, an evening in the **Chicago Hilton Hotel and Towers** (720 South Michigan Avenue, 312-922-4400 or 1-800-445-8667), in the top-of-the-line Conrad Hilton Suite, will run $6,000 a night. Pillow mints are complimentary. Every president since Truman has stayed here, along with major celebs like Frank Sinatra, Elizabeth Taylor, and Chicago's basketball god, Michael Jordan. At the **Hotel Inter-Continental** (505 North Michigan Avenue, 312-944-4100 or 1-800-628-2112), the pamper-your-ass accommodations are best in the bi-level Presidential Suite, which asks a much more reasonable $2,500 a night. The building is on the National Register of Historic Places, and even if you can't afford to stay here, you owe it to yourself to take a gander at the classic junior Olympic-sized swimming pool surrounded by majolica tiles — a reminder of when it was occupied by the old Medinah Athletic Club.

Okay, so you can't afford the terrycloth bathrobe sphere of luxury suites. How about spending just under $150 for a weeklong visit? The **J. Ira & Nicki Harris Family Hostel** (24 East Congress Parkway, 312-360-0300) is a member of **Hosteling International-American Youth Hostel**, a worldwide nonprofit organization. The hostel opened in 2000 in an old loft, built in 1886. It is also right in the thick of downtown Chicago, blocks from Buddy Guy's blues club (see "Secret Blues") and close to the Art Institute. Members of Hosteling International pay $19 for a shared room with two to three beds (no bath). Nonmembers pay $23 per night. Reservations are always recommended. If you would like to learn more about membership, click to www.hiayh.org. Membership in the organization gives you discounted access to 4,500 hostels in more than 70 countries.

If you want to stay downtown, reservations are essential. Because Chicago is a trade show Mecca with the massive **McCormick Place Complex** (2301 South Lake Shore Drive), rooms are often very hard to come by. The **Congress Plaza Hotel** (520 South Michigan Avenue, 312-427-3800 or 1-800-635-1666, single or double $119 to $165) is located right across from Grant Park. With early reservations in off-peak seasons, you can bag regular specials as low as $79. While not quite as decadent as the luxury hotels, this is still a nice overnight with plenty of history. Farther south, the **Best Western Grant Park Hotel** (1100 South Michigan Avenue, 312-922-2900) is a tidy, comfortable operation, with double occupancy room rates ranging from $99 to $159 a night. The **Red Roof Inn** (162 East Ontario Street, 312-787-3580, single $99, double $112) is a 16-story hotel just half a mile from all the action of Michigan Avenue. The **Quality Inn** (1 South Halsted Street, 312-829-5000, single $139, double $149) is just a few blocks west of downtown, right next to the Greek Town neighborhood (see "Secret Saganaki"), which runs along Halsted

Street from Madison Street to Van Buren Street. Another hotel just off Michigan Avenue is the **Best Western** (162 East Ohio Street, 312-787-3100), where rates range from $129 to $189 a night.

If you don't want to stay in the middle of all the downtown commotion, you can find some terrific bargains in other parts of the city, and even get a more honest taste of Chicago's spirit. The **Days Inn Near North** (644 West Diversey Avenue, 773-525-7010, single $89, double $119) is known to locals as the "rock 'n' roll Days Inn." Many touring bands have crashed here. It's a nice, clean hotel in the midst of a busy shopping district — and it's close to Wrigley Field. Just a block away, yet more rockers have stayed at the **Comfort Inn** (601 West Diversey Avenue, 773-348-2810, single $108, double $128). The **Willows Hotel** (555 West Surf Street, 773-528-8400 or 1-800-787-3108, single $139, double $179) is located in an artsy enclave of the Lakeview neighborhood. The Willows is surrounded by apartment buildings and residential homes, and is within walking distance of Lincoln Park and the Lincoln Park Zoo (see "Secret Kids"). The **Ramada Inn Lakeshore** (4900 South Lake Shore Drive, 773-288-5800, single $83, double $93) is directly across from a stretch of Lake Michigan that's unpopulated and tranquil. The hotel is near the University of Chicago, and lots of students stick Mom and Dad here during graduation. The Ramada is also popular with conventioneers and visiting academics.

If you have an adventurous heart and a meager billfold, travel to old Highway 41, North Lincoln Avenue, where you'll discover a strip of motor lodges well past their prime. Sure, more than a few light bulbs need to be replaced on the street-side signs, and you might get solicited by a prostitute or you might spy a crack deal going down in a parking lot. But the rooms are generally clean and safe. Here are just a few of the contenders: the **Summit Motel** (5308 North Lincoln

Avenue, 773-561-3762, single or double $50), the **Apache Motel** (5535 North Lincoln Avenue, 773-728-9400, single weekday $45, weekend $60; double weekday $50, weekend $70), and the **Lincoln Inn** (5952 North Lincoln Avenue, 773-784-1118, single weekday $45, weekend $55). I have stayed at a few of these places and besides a bloody mattress or two, riff-raff in the parking lots, and a couple of friendly insects, I walked out safe and sound.

SECRET
MARTINIS

While the retro-happy Rat Pack wannabes have watched the swing craze come and go, the cocktail culture lives on in Chicago. **Ivan's** (3358 North Ashland Avenue, 773-525-2140), a dark and friendly neighborhood bar, makes smashing martinis. They're nothing fancy, just straight-ahead jet fuel, James Bond style. This is my watering hole of choice. Weekends are uncomfortably crowded with Gen-xers, but on weeknights, Ivan's becomes a low-key lounge with DJs spinning everything from great alternative rock to old-time jazz to electronica. Look around for me. If I'm there, I'll buy you a drink. And if I'm not there, just admire the wallpaper. When they were rehabbing this place, the owners discovered a vintage '50s print buried underneath layers of paint and wood paneling.

For sheer selection, **Martini Ranch** (311 West Chicago Avenue, 312-335-9500) concocts nearly 50 different martinis, including one very good cosmopolitan. For a gigantic martini in a '40s supper-club setting, try **Club Lucky** (1824 West Wabansia Avenue, 773-227-2300). The

Italian food is pretty damned good too. My brand-new bar of choice is the **Tiny Lounge** (1814 West Addison Street, 773-296-9620). Gently upscale, candlelit, and quaint, this narrow little after-hours joint is nestled directly below the Brown Line elevated train tracks at the Addison stop. There's a vast menu of martinis, from fruity and sweet to hardboiled.

But the real environment, where martinis have never been part of some trendy fad, is the businessman's stomping ground — the hotel bar. Be it a two-martini lunch or a late-night libation, the **Salon** at the **Hotel Inter-Continental** (505 North Michigan Avenue, 312-944-4100 or 1-800-628-2122) serves up the best. It's chilled to icy perfection, always served with some left over, the shaker buried deep in a chrome-handled bucket of ice. At $8.95 a pop, it's a little exorbitant, but go ahead, treat yourself. Not far behind on the list of good hotel bar martinis is the concoction at the **Seasons Lounge** within the **Four Seasons Hotel** (120 East Delaware Place, 312-280-8800). There's also a cigar bar for you stogie aficionados.

Chicago's heavy hitters — local politicians and lawyers and CEOS — head to **Gibsons Steakhouse** (1028 North Rush Street, 312-266-8999), where the martinis are almost as huge as the steaks. Almost.

SECRET

MAXWELL MARKET

Gentrification spelled doom for the original **Maxwell Street Market**. At one point, this was the largest open-air market in the world. For nearly a century, this street-side bazaar was an explosion of people

selling all sorts of ratty junk. The old joke was that if your house got robbed, you could go down to Maxwell Street and buy it back. Televisions, musical instruments, jewelry, clothes, tube socks — you name it. But in September 1994, the market was relocated (thanks in large part to the growth of the University of Illinois) to an area a few blocks away. It's really kind of sad. It isn't even on Maxwell Street anymore. Today, you can find it every Sunday from dawn to mid-afternoon on Canal Street, between Roosevelt Road and 17th Street. The market is open year round. And while the newer incarnation only houses about half the vendors of the original, it's still a good start when your house gets burglarized — that is, if someone stole your tube socks. Go for the experience, the authentic Mexican fare like gorditas with grilled cactus, and the startup blues bands belting out old classics.

SECRET
MEAT MARKETS

If you thought this category was devoted to pickup joints, sorry to disappoint you. Chicago has a long history in the meatpacking industry. Chicago poet Carl Sandburg once called the city "the hog butcher to the world." At the industry's pinnacle, the Union Stock Yards on the city's South Side spanned a sprawling 475 acres and housed more than 100,000 cattle and hogs. Today, the Union Stock Yards may be gone (they were closed in 1971), but you can visit the last vestige of this important facet of Chicago's history at the old **Union Stock Yard Gate** (850 West Exchange Avenue). This rugged limestone gate once marked the entrance to the stockyards.

But even though the yards are gone, Chicagoans still celebrate their legacy by visiting neighborhood meat markets, where the Italian sausage will inspire you never to eat out at a restaurant again. Really. And the steaks . . . huge, lean fillets that are perfect on the grill on a fine summer evening. Anyway you cut it, Chicagoans love their meat, and their meat markets.

The **Paulina Market** (3501 North Lincoln Avenue, 773-248-6272) carries all sorts of excellent sausages. And with such large German, Italian, and Polish populations, Chicago must be a sausage town. How about a homemade brat or an apple pork sausage? It might be a bit on the expensive side here — a filet mignon wrapped in bacon runs $20 a pound — but it's worth the extra dough. There's also a well-stocked freezer section with venison and ostrich, and a cooler with leberkäse (German meatloaf). Walk into **Bornhofen's** (6155 North Broadway Street, 773-764-0714) and introduce yourself just once to the two old guys wearing the aprons and paper hats. They'll remember your name forever. And you'll remember the porterhouse steaks and potato sausage. At the **Halsted Packing House** (445 North Halsted Street, 312-421-5147), you pick the size of your chops and they cut it — right before your eyes. When it's time for seafood, wander into **Burhop's** (609 West North Avenue, 312-642-8600) for a massive selection of fresh fish flown in daily. From a perfect cut of mahi mahi to shrimp and salmon, Burhop's has it all.

SECRET
MEDIA

If you're an out-of-town visitor or a recent transplant to Chicago, all the media sources can be mighty overwhelming. It can take years to ferret out your favorite source for weather, the best place for traffic reports, and the best talk radio shows. Trying to find a good rock radio station or a good R&B station takes time, too — ditto for jazz and classical. And where do you turn for sports? What's the best local television newscast? Who are the newspaper columnists worth reading?

Have you ever noticed that when you rent a car, the presets on the radio have never been entered? It's all static, leaving you to keep one eye on the freeway and the other on the scan button. Better buckle up. When I rent a car, if I happen upon a good radio station, I always try to set it to the radio's memory. Well, if you're looking for all the cool media sources Chicago has to offer, you can take comfort. Just like I do with the rental car radio, I've entered them all right here, at your fingertips. And you're in good hands. I'm an unabashed media whore. Yes, this list is entirely subjective, but my opinions come from a lifetime of watching local TV, listening to local radio, and reading the local papers.

Let's start with the weather. No one in Chicago makes sense of the Windy City's schizophrenic climate better than **Tom Skilling**, chief meteorologist at WGN-TV (The WB, Channel 9). Every weekday at noon and 9 PM, Tom offers up what can only be described as daily mini-doctoral dissertations. The ever-earnest Skilling lives weather, loves weather, and knows weather. Chicago loves him.

If you're stuck in traffic on one of Chicago's perpetually clogged expressways, talk radio may be your only relief. It can often guide you toward more free-flowing thoroughfares. For regular traffic and weather updates, turn to **WBBM 780 AM**, where reports are given every 10 minutes "on the eights." But even then, sometimes the traffic is just so bad you have to surrender and sit. Need to be entertained? Here are a few of my local talk favorites.

"**848**," on Chicago's National Public Radio station **WBEZ 91.5 FM**, is a smart, savvy, magazine-format program covering local arts and culture, politics, religion, race relations, health, sports, and much more. What makes this show so listenable is its host, **Steve Edwards**, who is one of the best interviewers in town. He does his homework and it shows. Tune in Monday through Friday, 9:35 AM to 11 AM. By the way, the program's title comes from the radio station's street address, 848 East Grand Avenue, which is at Chicago's famous Navy Pier.

Roe Conn and Garry Meier, on **WLS 890 AM** weekdays from 2 PM to 6 PM, are a smart-ass talk team minus the lowbrow stupidity of so many radio comedians. Conn and Meier discuss world events as well as local issues with a sharp mix of irreverence and intelligence. That said, I do have a guilty pleasure . . . **Howard Stern**, found in Chicago, weekday mornings from 6 AM to 11 AM, on **WCKG 105.9 FM**. Sure, the regular parade of strippers and silicone implants is juvenile (this is probably why his TV show sucks), but when Howard is skewering a celebrity or discussing the news, there's no one on the radio who is more honest or hilarious.

Not interested in talk? For jazz aficionados, here are two well-kept secrets. While the signal is just 5,000 watts, the mission is mighty at **WDCB 90.9 FM**, a 24-hour-a-day, commercial-free station with one of the best program schedules in town. While the lineup is predominantly jazz, you'll also find world music, folk, bluegrass, and classical.

On Sunday afternoons from noon to 3 PM, tune into **WBEZ 91.5 FM** and listen to host **Dick Buckley** play what he calls "the good old good ones." As the motto implies, you won't find avant-garde jazz or nauseating "lite" jazz here, just the classics for three wonderful hours. Buckley knows his tunes — he's been spinning jazz disks for the station since 1977.

Rock listeners have a whole slew of selections up and down the Chicago radio dial, and most of them are unfettered corporate residuum. You can blame this on the mass of mergers, consolidations, and buy-outs by huge communications companies like Emmis and Bonneville. Now, nearly every playlist on every station sounds the same, and program directors, handcuffed by corporate memorandums, refrain from playing anything new, daring, or unknown. 'Tis a pity. Still, you can find some good rock 'n' roll on the airwaves.

The least corporate of the corporate-owned stations is **WXRT 93.1 FM**, where you'll get everything from authentic Chicago blues to punk to classic rock. Still, ever since this station was snapped up in a corporate buyout a few years back, it has consistently waxed wimpy.

In the mornings, with the glut of testosterone-heavy talk radio, landing on a station that actually plays music can be a miracle. If all you want to do is rock in the morning, try out **WXCD 94.7 FM**, which touts itself as "the new alternative." Morning woman **Brooke Hunter** is perfect for this time slot. She's cool and energetic without sounding like she's just guzzled a six-pack of Red Bull, like most morning personalities. She also plays a good mix of rock, from the Foo Fighters to Weezer. Nothing too risky, just good rock.

Of course, if you're looking for the real pantheon of obscure, cool, and unsigned bands, you tune to college radio. Check out Northwestern University's **WNUR 89.3 FM**. Each weekday from 2 PM to 10 PM, the station's "**Rock Show**" showcases all sorts of independent, experimental, and local rock. Another station that serves up bleeding-edge rock is WLUW **88.7 FM**, Loyola University's radio station. The playlist here has multiple personalities, including Korean pop, local alternative rock, reggae, drum 'n' bass, and ambient music. Also, no commercials!

For fans of R&B and hip-hop, turn to WGCI **107.5 FM**. This station is seriously caffeinated — pumped up on high-energy music from morning to night. For Top 40 dance, spin the dial to WBBM **96.3 FM**.

For years, Chicago has made the 10 PM news on WLS-TV (ABC, Channel 7) number one in the ratings. The station's sportscaster, **Mark Giangreco,** is arguably the best on the tube. He's honest and straightforward, and he avoids throwing around all those ESPN-influenced look-how-clever-I-can-be catchphrases. But if you want really outstanding sports coverage, read *Sun-Times* columnist **Rick Telander**. This guy is a regular on all those annual best American sports writing lists and he deserves it. He's thoughtful, smart, and even profound, a real throwback to an era when sports journalists were some of the best ink-slingers around.

But now, back to the 10 o'clock news. In my opinion, the local Chicago news is mostly dumbed down with too many silly food segments, the requisite health and medicine report, and goofy weathermen who ought to be on an improv stage. That said, for the smartest local television, turn to "**Chicago Tonight**" on WTTW-TV (PBS, Channel 11). Host **Phil Ponce** reviews the news with an intelligence and insight utterly uncommon on the tube. The show usually focuses on one topic per episode, with a roundtable discussion moderated by Ponce. Guests come from all walks of Chicago life and the conversations are always in-depth and entertaining.

Of course, there's nothing like good old-fashioned print journalism for insight into a city and its news. Chicago has several newspaper columnists worth checking out. The ***Sun-Times'* Roger Ebert** may be world famous as a Pulitzer Prize–winning film critic (the only one in the prestigious award's history), but he often writes thoughtful op-ed pieces that always get people talking. **Richard Roeper**, who replaced the late, legendary Gene Siskel, is now Ebert's partner on the popular syndicated television show "**Ebert and Roeper: At the Movies**." By day, Roeper, a native of the city's South Side, is a daily columnist for the ***Sun-Times***, and he writes with panache and wit about the day's issues.

For media coverage (this section is for media junkies, after all), check out **Michael Miner** in the ***Chicago Reader*** (see "Secret Periodicals"). Miner's weekly column, "**Hot Type**," is one of the best reads around. Whenever the media make news, Miner is usually the one to break the story.

Of course, a subjective list like this wouldn't be complete without a tip of the hat to my friend and all-time favorite newspaperman, **Rick Kogan** (see "Secret Rick Kogan"), a senior writer for the ***Chicago Tribune***. For a slice of pure, sweet, honest-to-goodness Chicago, pick up his weekly column "**Sidewalks**" in the *Tribune*'s Sunday magazine. Rick is, very simply, a wonderful writer. You can also hear him every Sunday morning on his eclectic, top-rated radio show, "**The Sunday Papers**," which airs on WGN 720 AM from 6:30 AM to 9 AM.

SECRET
MEXICAN

When I was a kid, every few years my mom used to buck Thanksgiving and Christmas traditions by preparing ethnic feasts instead of

adhering to the predictable turkey, cranberry, and stuffing routine. One of my favorites of her holiday meals was Mexican. She would travel to the Mexican market and buy freshly made corn tortillas and stuff them with boiled shredded beef that sat and simmered atop the stove all day long. The meat was perfectly seasoned and would fill the house with heavenly aromas. She would top the enchiladas with heaps of melted cheese, spicy homemade nortena sauce, green chives, chilies, and cilantro. To this day, I love Mexican food and Mexican culture. When my mom passed away in 1992, her recipe went with her. I've never had enchiladas that good since. But I've been looking . . .

In Chicago, Mexican restaurants dot the landscape almost as frequently as fire hydrants. But honestly, most of them are mediocre at best — just a notch above Taco Bell. But with the taste buds and the nose for a fine Mexican meal, I have sniffed out a few outstanding exceptions here and there.

The **Pilsen** neighborhood (bounded by 16th Street, Halsted Street, the Chicago River, and Damen Avenue) is home to Chicago's Mexican arts community. This is where you should begin your quest *para todos las cosas authenticas mexicanas*. Originally settled by German and Irish immigrants in the 1860s, Pilsen earned its name when Czechs and Poles arrived in the 1920s. But ever since the middle of the century, it has been an area steeped in Hispanic culture.

Visit Pilsen on a cold winter's day. Bundle up well, with a hat and scarves and gloves. Burrow your face deep in a warm jacket. You'll still be able to inhale and take in the smell of grilled meat, spices, and homemade tortillas. A big contributor to this aromatic aesthetic is **Cuernavaca** (1160 West 18th Street, 312-829-1147), perhaps the most authentic restaurant in the area. It has the right atmosphere, with colorful murals on the walls, Spanish-tiled floors, and animal skulls hanging over the bar. But the real treat here is the chow. Start off with a Mexican beer or one of the frothy margaritas, and then dig into traditional temptations like fajitas or enchiladas. If you have a hefty appetite, the costillas al carbon (that's "barbecued ribs" *en Ingles*) are the house specialty. Spiced to perfection, the tender meat just falls off the bone. For the more intrepid, there are spicy brain and beef tongue entrées.

If you head west down Pilsen's main drag, 18th Street, you can't miss **Nuevo Leon** (1515 West 18th Street, 312-421-1517), with a façade exploding in bright, washed colors. Since 1962, the same family has been running this neighborhood restaurant. With a vast menu serving everything from enchiladas drenched in chocolate mole sauce to pork tamales and menudo (tripe soup), Nuevo is well loved by locals. Other favorites include the chili relleno de queso o picadillo and the milanesa de res (deep-fried steak).

When you're done eating, the neighborhood beckons, with its numerous colorful murals and shops filled with all kinds of Mexican splendors.

The only Mexican museum in the entire Midwest is just a short distance away. This is a fine place to soak in some culture while digesting your feast. The **Mexican Fine Arts Center Museum** (1852 West 19th Street, 312-738-1503) displays world-class exhibits of local, national, and international artists. The permanent collection holds works by celebrated Mexican artists such as Diego Rivera, José Orozco, and graphic artist Francisco Toledo. The museum also schedules a myriad of lectures, classes, and performances throughout the year. But the biggest draw for the MFACM each year is the energetic **Dia de los Muertos** (Day of the Dead) festival, held every September. As tradition goes, each autumn, monarch butterflies that have summered in the US and Canada return to Mexico for the winter. The locals welcome back the butterflies, which they believe bear the spirits of their departed. These spirits are honored during Dia de los Muertos, a colorful and joyous fiesta alive with music, visual arts, dancing skeletons and ghouls, and just all-around good cheer.

Of course, Pilsen does not have a copyright on Mexican culture. Searching for a killer margarita? By far, the most infamous in Chicago can be found at **El Jardin** (3335 North Clark Street, 773-528-6775), where the fishbowl-sized glasses are loaded with so much booze, I promise, you won't leave sober. Seriously, I have seen the hardest drinkers fall prey to these things. Grown men taking naps in corners are common sights. I've even known an alcoholic who claims these things sent him to rehab. They don't call them "Mind Bombs" for nothing. If you happen into this 32-year-old family-run restaurant on a weekend night, you'll meet the nicest host in the world. His name is Joe. Tell him I sent you and he'll set you up.

Just up the block, the **Texas Star Fajita Bar** (3365 North Clark Street, 773-975-8008) is a favorite with the frat-boy crowd, but don't hold that against the place. The food here is exceptional Tex-Mex fare. My favorite is the black bean burrito. Order it with diced jalapeños for an extra kick. The frozen margaritas here are blended and stored in a Slurpee-style machine, which ensures perfect consistency and superb taste. This place would give the Galloping Gourmet a hard-on except for the fact that the really tasty chips and really tasty salsa cost extra. What the hell is that? Don't you hate a Mexican restaurant that charges for these standard table-top starters? You ain't gonna get this kind of honesty in one of those corporate travel guides. Aren't you glad you bought this book?

For incredible sopa de frijol negros, (black bean soup), head to **Lindo Mexico** (2638 North Lincoln Avenue, 773-871-4832), where the portions are generous and the atmosphere conjures up an Oaxacan market. The place offers "heart-smart" choices, a rarity on Mexican menus.

The light, crisp, not-too-greasy chips go wonderfully with the fresh salsa that has just the right kick and a whole lot of cilantro.

For authentic, upscale Mexican dishes made by a white guy (go figure), try **Frontera Grill** and **Topolobampo** (445 North Clark Street, 312-661-1434). These connected sister restaurants are owned and operated by Rick Bayless, host of the popular culinary television program "Mexico One Plate at a Time." Scrumptious favorites include the guacamole with pieces of cucumber, radish, and jicama; spicy shrimp tacos; and pork chilorio — a Mexican pulled pork entrée. Expect long lines and big crowds.

And let me whisper one last glorious Mexican restaurant recommendation in your ear. **Taqueria El Asadero** (2213 West Montrose Avenue, 773-583-5563) is a small, storefront hole-in-the-wall with a grill that's always sizzling and steaming with bell peppers and onions, skirt steak and chicken. The food here is super cheap, the service is fast and friendly, and the tacos are that good. A couple can gorge here for under 10 bucks. And don't forget to order a bottle of cold Mexican tamarind soda.

SECRET
MOVIES

❧

Like any large city, Chicago has about three gazillion multiplexes with screens the size of those handheld Sony Watchmans and sound that is worse. That's a bit hyperbolic, but it's almost true. The rub is that a movie in one of these theaters costs $8.75. At least that's cheaper than the $9.50 ticket at New York's Loews Theaters. If you want to head to one of these big houses, simply check the Friday entertainment sections of the *Tribune* or the *Sun-Times*, or look at the film listings in *New City* or the *Chicago Reader* (see "Secret Periodicals").

Many of the grand old movie palaces from Chicago's yesteryear have been demolished. But some have remained, such as the **Uptown** (Broadway Street and Lawrence Avenue), which opened in 1925. Back then, it was the second-largest theater in the country, a baby sister to New York's Radio City Music Hall. Today, it sits dilapidated and silent, awaiting its fate. In its heyday, the theater — with its elaborate Spanish Renaissance décor, chandeliered lobby, and 5000-seat auditorium — was the North Side's crowning jewel. It once housed the most expensive Wurlitzer built in that period. As they say, those were the days. Over the years, this huge and ornate cinema has changed ownership several times, but no one has been able to revive it. Part of the problem is that the Uptown is located in an economi-cally depressed neighborhood. But recently, with the winds of gentrification gusting, it seems likely that will change. The old Uptown, I predict, will rise again.

Fortunately, the **Music Box Theater** (3733 North Southport Avenue, 773-871-6604), built four years after the Uptown, still draws crowds. The theater is the première art house in the city, presenting an average of 300 films a year. Its architectural style stands nearly unchanged to this day. It is an eclectic mix of Italian and Spanish décor. The dark blue, cove-lit ceiling features twinkling stars and moving clouds, and the plaster ornamentation evokes an Italian court-yard. It's unique. And here's a festive way to celebrate the holidays: see the movie classics *White Christmas* and *It's a Wonderful Life* at the Music Box, which presents them starting the week before Christmas. Included is a mad, sassy carol sing-along accompanied by the house organ.

Facets Multimedia (1517 West Fullerton Avenue, 773-281-4114) has two screening rooms for film, video, and live performance. The screens are small and the sound is unimpressive. But the lineup of obscure, small-budget indies, classics, and foreign films is unparalleled. Screen retrospectives of major directors, along with new and pristine prints of classics, are also shown. And if you wander down into the basement, you will discover an absurd number of foreign videotapes for rental. Peruse the shelves and you'll find Spanish, Middle Eastern, British, Japanese, Scandinavian, Australian, French, and Italian films among many other gems from cinema-producing countries.

Another cinema for independent, art, and alternative film is the **Gene Siskel Film Center** (164 North State Street, 312-846-2800), which has a selection that changes daily. There's a strong schedule of art films, along with retrospectives of directors. The center also hosts occasional lectures by critics and filmmakers.

For second-run films or long-awaited releases of foreign, art, and classic films, try the **Three Penny Cinema** (2424 North Lincoln Avenue, 773-935-5744). The floors are a catch basin of goopy candy and other mystery fluids, and the seats are a bit battered, but the films are top notch. For a slightly off-price cinema in a quaint Chicago neighborhood, visit the **Davis Theater** (4614 North Lincoln Avenue, 773-784-0893), where you can catch big-budget features for just seven bucks. For you early birds, the first show of the day is $5.

And for an evening of troglodyte behavior, you might want to investigate the **Brew & View at the Vic** (3145 North Sheffield Avenue, 312-618-8439). The **Vic Theatre** has long been a music venue, hosting national touring musicians who are too big to play a club but not big enough to land a ballroom gig. But on music-free weekends, the place turns into a rowdy movie house, screening lots of cult favorite films and serving up a healthy dose of beer. It's a good deal: $5 gets you three movies.

S E C R E T
MUSEUMS

When you visit Chicago, most people, including me, will tell you to visit the Art Institute or the Field Museum or the Shedd Aquarium. Wonderful, every one of them. But Chicago plays host to a score of lesser-known and very beguiling museums. Put on your walking shoes.

I always recommend the **Chicago Historical Society** (1601 North Clark Street, 312 642-4600) to anyone who wants to get in touch with, as poet Carl Sandburg called it, "City of the Big Shoulders." The CHS is far less of a tourist trap than the aforementioned institutions, but it is every bit as fascinating and educational. And that doesn't mean it's a snoozefest for the kids, either. You'll find lots here for everyone between the womb and the tomb. For research or for fun, explore the prints and photographs collection — one of the largest image collections in the United States that's accessible to the public free of charge. There are 1.5 million images in all. Here, stored away and waiting to be handled with white gloves, are photos of the Civil War, famous Chicagoans, movie stars like Charlie Chaplin (a short-term Chicago resident), and more that relates to the city. There are old street scenes and cityscape pictures of Wrigley Field when it was known as "Weeghman Park." The CHS also has an immense collection of slavery and emancipation materials, including an original copy of the 13th Amendment, which freed the slaves. Everything here has a Chicago bent and many exhibits are interactive (a plus for parents). There's no better way to learn about this amazing city on the lake.

For something completely different, the **Oriental Institute Museum** (1155 East 58th Street, 773-702-9521) is a showcase of the history, art, and archaeology of the ancient Near East. As part of the University of Chicago, which has supported research and archaeological excavation in the Near East since 1919, the museum exhibits major collections of antiquities from Egypt, Mesopotamia, Iran, Syria, Palestine, and Anatolia. You can take a virtual tour of the museum at its Web site at www.oi.uchicago.edu/OI/MUS/OI_Museum.html. But why screw around on the Web? This place is off the path of most tourists and it's free.

The **Museum of Holography** (1134 West Washington Street, 312-226-1007) is a small museum devoted entirely to laser-generated, three-dimensional artwork like holographs. The images, from Michael Jordan to a great white shark, simply leap from the walls. This is the only museum in the country strictly dedicated to holography. Admission is $4 for adults, free for children under six. But don't visit on Mondays or Tuesdays — it's closed.

Here are few more off-the-radar museums. The largest ethnic museum in the country is the **Polish Museum of America** (984 North Milwaukee Avenue, 773-384-3352). Exhibits include Polish paintings, sculptures, costumes, and folk art. The **National Vietnam Veterans Art Museum** (1801 South Indiana Avenue, 312, 326-0270) features an extensive fine arts collection of paintings, sketches, sculpture, and photography by veterans of the war. The **Hemingway Museum** (200 North Oak Park Avenue, Oak Park, 708-848-2222) focuses on the first 20 years of Papa's life, showcasing letters, photographs, and early writings. Any fan of the author will love it. And just a block away, you Hemingway enthusiasts can visit his birthplace, at the **Hemingway Home** (339 North Oak Park Avenue, Oak Park).

SECRET
NAVIGATION

You can't get lost in Chicago. The City on the Prairie was built using a grid pattern. Just remember this: the address numbering system starts downtown at State Street and Madison Street and crawls north, south, east, and west. If you are at the United Center, for example, at 1901 West Madison Street, and you walk 19 blocks east, you will be back at State and Madison. It's that easy. Each block represents 100. There are a few diagonal thoroughfares, but not many, and those really come in handy as short cuts (see "Secret Shortcuts"). And the old Chicago adage is true — the lake is always east.

SECRET
NEIGHBORHOOD BARS

They are the kinds of places where neon beer signs flickering in the windows cut through a blanket of midnight snowfall like a lighthouse beacon. They are the kinds of places where the front door is propped open in the summertime, a bank of laughter spilling out atop a gauzy cloud of tar and nicotine. They are the kinds of places where, indeed, the bartender learns your name on your first visit and

remembers it. They have jukeboxes and dart boards, corner TVs, and tap beer that's really nothing to write home about. Most of all, they have character — the kind of character that is as thick and scarred as the coating of wax layered atop their dark mahogany bars. While one of the city's official mottoes is "the city of neighborhoods," I'd like to make an editorial correction. Chicago is "the city of neighborhood taverns." Just walk a few blocks down any street in just about any pocket of the city, from Beverly to Bucktown, and you'll find a corner bar where you're always welcome. With so many great little secret taverns to choose from, this list is by no means complete. These are just a few suggestions to get you started. If you find your own favorite quaint watering hole, let me know about it.

G&L **Fire Escape** (2157 West Grace Street, 773-472-1138) is a dark den in the St. Ben's neighborhood. Amidst the rows of red brick two-flats and looming trees, you'll find this one-room bar, named for the local firemen who frequent it. Plumbers, electricians, and cops come here, too. People drink domestic beer served cold and in the can. They do have Irish drafts and a German beer or two. You talk here. You watch a ball game with your friends. It really doesn't matter what you do for a living.

The **Hop Leaf** (5148 North Clark Street, 773-334-9851) succeeds greatly where neighborhood taps should: it mirrors the neighborhood around it. In this smoky Andersonville bar, you'll find a diverse and affluent mix of people, just like Andersonville itself. There's a vibrant mix of students, gays and lesbians, and actors from nearby storefront theaters, and business folks with their ties loosened and their sleeves rolled up. And with more than 100 beers to choose from, you can't go wrong.

Woodlawn Tap (1172 East 55th Street, 773-643-5516) is the tavern of choice for University of Chicago students and faculty. Here, the intellectual disputes flow as freely as the beer. For over 50 years, owner Jimmy Wilson ran this storied, ragged pub, which was a favorite stop for writer Saul Bellow. Jimmy died in February 1999. Raise a glass.

Tuman's Alcohol Abuse Center (2159 West North Avenue, no telephone) is the kind of tavern you wouldn't know existed except for the fact that I just gave you the address. Dark, smoky, and discreet, this place is an artist's sanctuary, but you'll also run into scores of businessmen and bikers. Big plus: this is one hell of a cheap place to drink.

If you have a long layover at Midway Airport, wander several blocks south to **Mr. C's** (4654 West 63rd Street, 773-582-0833) where, late at night, off-duty pilots, flight attendants, and baggage handlers unwind from the roar of the runway. During the day, you'll find long-suffering White Sox fans from the predominantly Polish neighborhood nearby commiserating over beers. The jukebox has a mix of good standards, and the owner, Andy Chilmon, is a heck of a nice guy.

The problem with most secret places is that they don't remain secrets for long. That's the conundrum of writing a book of this sort. I'm spilling the beans on many places that are wonderful because they are lesser known or out of the way or frequented by locals. One of these hidden treasures, already discovered by the masses but well worth a mention nonetheless, is **Guthrie's** (1300 West Addison Street, 773-477-2900). A decade ago, this inviting tavern was a place to mellow out with your friends. There was a sizeable shelf stacked with board games: Monopoly, Risk, Scrabble, and the like. The place spun soft music, old jazz, or the Grateful Dead. And then it was discovered. Weekends at Guthrie's are wall to wall, but during the week you can still get a table and not have to raise your voice to be heard.

Here's my favorite neighborhood bar of all, but you have to drive about half an hour north of downtown to reach it: **Meier's Tavern** (235 East Lake Avenue, Glenview, 847-724-0477). It's worth the drive. Meier's opened in 1933 in an old white farmhouse. It has not changed much since then. The beers on tap and in the bottle are good, solid beers — no tutti-frutti microbrews here. And the food is reliable standard fare, too: sandwiches served with tater tots or fries, with ketchup and mustard set out in packets. A game invariably flickers away on the corner televisions. Gangsters used to come here. Local sports celebrities still drop in to get away from it all.

SECRET
NEWSSTANDS

The spot in Chicago with the largest selection of out-of-town newspapers and magazines, ranging from pubescent periodicals (*Tiger Beat*) and conspiracy rags (*UFO Magazine*) to imported music (*Kerrang!*) and porn (*Leg Show*), is the **City Newsstand** (4018 North Cicero Avenue, 773-545-7377). This venerable operation — which, at last tally, carried more than 6,000 periodicals — is in the Old Irving Park neighborhood, where metered parking is accessible. One quarter affords you an hour of browsing time. Perhaps the best non-adult bookstore for porn is **World News** (3121 North Broadway Street, 773-477-4568). The selection caters to the most deviant of fetishes. But be careful: the shop owner, looming behind his counter, gets hot under the collar if you browse the porn section without putting down a $1 down payment. But once you put down the dollar, he leaves you alone, and your money is even refundable toward your pornographic purchase. World News also carries a vast selection of regular magazines and comic books. Chicago has two **Tower Records/Books/Video** stores (2301 North Clark Street, 773-477-5994; 214 South Wabash Avenue, 312-987-9044). The Clark Street location carries a huge selection of out-of-town newspapers and free periodicals (see "Secret Periodicals"), as well as a big supply of fanzines (see "Secret 'Zines").

SECRET
NICHE BOOKSTORES

With the arrival of the superstores in the last decade, little independent booksellers have scrambled and foraged to stay alive. But even with all the Barnes and Noble and Borders operations in the Chicagoland area, several little book nooks have succeeded and — in a few cases — thrived quite nicely. A handful of wonderful niche bookstores exist, specializing in genres and categories to combat the mega-square-foot superstores with their giant discounts and cappuccino machines.

The **Savvy Traveler** (310 South Michigan Avenue, 312-913-9800), located in the heart of downtown on the Mag Mile, is the perfect place to plan a honeymoon to Bora Bora or a family road trip to the Wisconsin Dells. This is the best store in town for picking up maps, foreign-language books, and city guides — not to mention those handy AC adapters that fit into wall sockets in different countries, and other cool gadgets for all your travel needs. Bon voyage!

Another fabulous travel shop is **Hit The Road** (3758 North Southport Avenue, 773-388-8338). Here, you can jet, drive, hike, tour, or journey to your heart's content. The shop is small, but the selection of books and travel knickknacks is irresistible. The shelves are stocked with guidebooks that circumnavigate the globe, travel essays that ponder the trip, and postcards and artwork that will remind you of the voyage for years to come. Extremely neat stuff.

Theater enthusiasts will love **Act 1** (2540 North Lincoln Avenue, 312-348-675, www.act1books.com), which sells hard-to-find theatrical material. When Chicago actors need monologues for auditions, this is where they come.

Centuries and Sleuths (743 Garfield Street, Oak Park, 708-848-7243), located on the outskirts of Chicago, caters to armchair detectives and history buffs. It has one of the best and most complete Chicago history sections anywhere. The seats are so comfortable that you can't help but hunker down with the complete works of Sir Arthur Conan Doyle. Looking for a little instant karma? **Transitions Bookplace** (1000 West North Avenue, 312-951-READ) is the city's New Age touchstone, offering up all the self-help advice and chakra-cleansing tips your inner child could ever pray for. The store also hosts an incredible array of wellness seminars in the nearby **Transitions Learning Center** (1750 North Kingsbury Street, 312-951-READ). For a gigantic selection of Jewish material — thousands of titles in both Hebrew and English — check out the 23-year-old **Chicago Hebrew Bookstore** (2942 West Devon Avenue, 773-973-6636). One more quirky little left-field (so to speak) store is **Revolution Books** (3449 North Sheffield Avenue, 773-528-5353), which stocks a bevy of Maoist titles. The **Occult Bookstore** (1561 North Milwaukee Avenue, 773-292-0995) resembles a spooky dream — dusty rare books sit on the shelves, occult paintings hang on the walls, and incense, oils, and candles burn in the nooks. The book collection includes rarities like *Spiritual and Demonic Magick*.

While it's not really fair to call a foreign-language store a "niche bookstore" per se, I'd be remiss in not mentioning **Libreria Giron** (1443 West 18th Street, 312-226-1406), a wonderful family-owned Spanish bookstore in the *corazon* of the Pilsen neighborhood.

The US **Government Bookstore** (401 South State Street, 312-353-5133) is a one-stop shop for a bizarre variety of federal government publications. Here, you'll discover titles on everything from taxation to representation. There are books on national parks, education, and the census data.

True Lincoln buffs will appreciate the 70-year-old **Abraham Lincoln Bookstore** (357 West Chicago Avenue, 312-944-3085). This shop specializes in what storeowner Dan Weinberg calls "Lincolniana." The store stocks nearly 3,500 titles related to Honest Abe. Civil War freaks flock to this cozy River North shop from all corners of the nation to buy hard-to-find reference books, documents, and biographies.

And finally . . . these days, every Barnes and Noble and Borders bookstore stocks row after row of science fiction books. But no store in Chicago can come within a light year of **Stars Our Destination** (705 Main Street, Evanston, 847-570-5925). The shop, which houses more than 6,000 new science fiction titles and at least 24,000 used SF titles, is a sci-fi fan's fantasy come true.

SECRET

OLDEST PROFESSION

It's true, you know. In a sprawling metropolis like Chicago, you can find just about anything you might want. You just have to know where to look. Really. And that's where a book like this comes in handy — to point you in the right direction. So, hypothetically, let's just assume that you were interested in finding a little, shall we say, romantic companionship for the evening, or the afternoon, or the morning, for that matter. Here's where to look.

The back pages of the *Chicago Reader* and *New City* (see "Secret Periodicals") are loaded with ads for "escorts" and "massage services" that make house calls. But picking one out of the multitude of classified and display ads, no matter how sultry the language, is a crapshoot. This is how the routine works: you dial the number from the advertisement. On the other end of the line, you usually get a mysterious and sexy voice that prompts you to leave your number or to enter a numeric page. You hang up and you wait a few moments thinking, "What the hell am I doing?" and then your telephone rings. You pick up and the person on the other end explains the rates and asks for your address. They will never tell you over the phone that they engage in sexual activities. And you shouldn't inquire about sex over the phone either. This is part of the crapshoot. You don't know if you're talking to police Sergeant O'Malley on the other end, and they don't know who you are, either. So, you agree to the rates and give the person your address. Usually within an hour, your doorbell rings and your guest has arrived. They always come with an escort — some sort of bulky bodyguard for protection — who waits out in the car. Once the "massage therapist" has arrived, read the situation. Trust your instincts. This person in your house is probably not a cop. Probably. The final part of the crapshoot is what your masseuse will and will not do. Some only offer "hand massages." This can be kind of a letdown, so to speak, but that's the way it goes. The odds are good you'll have a special time with your new special friend, who will, most likely, leave you with a smile on your face.

Of course, this isn't the only way to solicit an escort or massage therapist or new friend. You can go out looking for one.

Even on the most bitterly cold winter nights at three in the morning, when the wind is slapping Chicago silly, creatures of the night parade along North Avenue near the 24-hour **Home Depot** (1232 West North Avenue, 773-486-9200). Look for them along the bridge that stretches over the Chicago River.

When conventions are in town at the **McCormick Place Complex** (2301 South Lake Shore Drive), you can often find even more fun-loving friends parading down Cermak Road. With well over four million trade show and convention visitors coming to Chicago each year, the escorts are kept busy. McCormick is a big place and after a long trade show day, you're tired and achy. Thank goodness you can always find a massage in Chicago to take all your tensions away.

SECRET
OLFACTORY

Chicago smells. Even when the city has been encased in a long streak of gray winter days, when it seems as though all things have frozen solid, the nostrils still detect life in Chicago. Outside the **Gonella**

Bread Factory (2002 West Erie Street, 312-733-2020), the sweet smell of sourdough drifts through the air. In the **Hubbard Street Tunnel** (Hubbard Street and the Kennedy Expressway), the perfume of chocolate flutters from a nearby candy factory. On the **El platforms**, the acidic snarl of the electric rails lingers over the tracks. Along **Lake Street**, the tang of sausage wafts from the meat markets. Outside **Gino's East** (160 East Superior Street, 312-943-1124), the scent of warm pizza dough snakes down the street. On **Canal Street**, diesel exhaust hangs from the stacks of idling tractor-trailers. And along the **Stevenson Expressway**, fresh, hot asphalt shoveled into potholes steams skyward. Chicago smells.

S E C R E T
OUTLETS
❧

What do department stores do with all their discontinued, irregular, or overstocked items? They send them to their outlets.

The **Gap Factory Outlet** (2778 North Milwaukee Avenue, 773-252-0594) stocks Gap duds for the entire family, with leftovers from its numerous Gap and Baby Gap stores. This is a really good place to pick up a pair of blue jeans for dirt cheap. For men, a notch up the formalwear ladder from the Gap is the **Mark Shale Outlet** (2593 North Elston Avenue, 773-772-9600). Here, you'll find well-made suits and sport coats at bargain prices. The **Burlington Coat Factory** (4520 South Damen Avenue, 773-254-0054; 7340 West Foster Avenue, 773-763-6006) carries — surprise, surprise — rack after rack of coats for all seasons. It has everything from winter parkas and trench coats to windbreakers and leathers. And it has aisles of housewares and deeply discounted linens, not to mention clothes for men, women, and children. If you suffer from the same form of shoe worship that plagued former Philippine First Lady Imelda Marcos, or if you just need a new pair of shoes, then head to the **Nine West Outlet** (2739 North Clark Street, 773-281-9132) for an extensive selection of women's footwear.

An obscure but cool shop for shutterbugs is **Central Camera Company** (230 South Wabash Avenue, 312-427-5580). This classic Chicago shop has been serving photography professionals and camera enthusiasts since 1899. Shoehorned into a tiny space and jam packed with film, cameras, tripods, bags, flashes, and binoculars in glass cases and on floor-to-ceiling shelves, this store — with its great neon sign out front — offers its wares at discounted prices.

If you're planning to entertain on a large scale, **Edward Don Company Outlet** (2525 North Elston Avenue, 773-489-7739) sells restaurant supplies to the public at super-reasonable prices. When I got married, we tried to do as much ourselves as possible, and this place came through in a big way. It stocks a huge supply of glassware, utensils, serving dishes, and candle holders — just about anything you could imagine for your big bash.

The **Wonder Hostess Bakery Thriftshop** (1301 West Diversey Avenue, 773-281-6700), a kid's sugar fantasy come true, stocks Hostess morsels at half price, including Twinkies and all four flavors of Hostess fruit pies (apple, cherry, lemon, and the hard-to-find blueberry). You can also pick up a quarter-pound loaf of Wonder Bread for just 36 cents, or a loaf of beefsteak rye (usually over $2 at the supermarket) for 79 cents.

If you have a green thumb, then you're probably familiar with **Smith & Hawken**, a catalog company based out of Mill Valley, California.

It carries something for gardeners of all passions. But you don't have to wait for the mail to arrive to enjoy the lush world of Smith & Hawken. There's an outlet store in Chicago (1780 North Marcey Street, 312-266-3666). Stocked with quality tools, flowering plants, seeds, pots, work wear, books, and furniture, it sells overstock from the catalog at a substantial discount.

S E C R E T
PAPER ARTS

The art of hand papermaking is enjoying a bold renaissance. Artists are discovering new and stunning ways to craft paper from scratch, using decorative elements like flower petals and fibers mixed into the pulp itself. After seeing these works of art, you'll never look at paper in quite the same way. But the resurgence in the medium doesn't just end there. Hand bookbinding is a hot fad, too. People are constructing their own books: accordion books, pop-up books, and traditional books using sewing, lining, and lightweight hard covers. And they're using unconventional materials like metal and plush velvet and rivets and rhinestones to cover them. It's all very cool.

At the **Columbia College Chicago Center for Book and Paper Arts** (1104 South Wabash Avenue, 312-344-6630), MFA and MA graduate degrees are offered, along with continuing education courses for those who are curious about this intriguing art form but realize that getting a job with an advanced degree in papermaking would be as likely as winning the lottery. Founded in 1992, the school has grown dramatically every year. Today, it has a gallery, a papermaking studio, a bindery, and a letterpress studio. There is also a resource room loaded with reference books and hundreds of delicate brass tools used for decorating books.

One of the hippest shops in the city is the **Paper Source** (232 West Chicago Avenue, 312-337-0798). Housed in an old three-story Victorian building, it carries everything you need to pour your own paper. And if you don't want to make paper yourself, the shop sells ready-made sheets in hundreds of designs, weights, colors, and textures. It's a heavenly stationery store. There are also bookbinding materials, how-to books on the papermaking arts, rubber stamps, and an entire area devoted to wedding invitations and wedding guest-books. The Paper Source conducts workshops in silk screening, calligraphy, and papermaking, too. Across the street, at **Pearl Art & Craft Supplies** (225 West Chicago Avenue, 312-915-0200), you'll discover still more papermaking materials, along with a wealth of other art supplies, including watercolor, oil and acrylic paints, linoleum blocks, canvas, silk-screening supplies, and reams of beautiful paper.

SECRET
PARKS

We Chicagoans love our parks. In total, there are over 7,400 acres of open green space, 29 miles of Lake Michigan shoreline, 520 parks, 800 baseball fields, 250 field houses, 90 swimming pools, and 10 Olympic-sized ice-skating rinks. In fact, the Chicago Park District is one of the most extensive municipal park systems in the world. And it's the one facet of Chicago government that really seems to do

its job and do it well. No tales of corruption. No heated bureaucratic arguments.

The crown jewel of the Chicago park system, if for no other reason than its location, is **Grant Park** (Randolph Street to Roosevelt Road along Lake Michigan, 312-747-6620). With Buckingham Fountain as its grand water-and-marble centerpiece, Grant Park covers 304 acres in total. In the summer, there's always some festival going on here, so if you're looking for something to do, you're in luck. The view of downtown (almost directly overhead) is breathtaking.

But in my estimation, Chicago's secret treasure is **Jackson Park** (6401 South Stony Island Avenue, 312-747-6187). Nestled south of the Museum of Science and Industry, the park was built, plotted, and planted to house the 1893 World's Columbian Exposition. There are lagoons for swimming and casting out a fishing line, and it also has the city's only 18-hole golf course. In the winter, this picturesque 500-acre grassland is a fabulous place to cross-country ski. The most impressive part of Jackson Park is its entrance, where you will find a massive statue of Columbia, which loomed over the 1893 exposition. Along with the Museum of Science and Industry, this is one of the last historical reminders of the great fair of more than a century ago.

For a secret swimming spot, my choice is the Olympic-sized pool in **Hamlin Park** (312-742-7785). Even on scorching summer days, there's hardly anyone here. Sometimes you even have the whole pool to yourself. Contact the park for information on free swim hours. This won't remain a secret for long.

For a quiet walk, visit **River Park** (5100 North Francisco Avenue, 773-742-7516), a North Side treasure hidden from tourists. The centerpiece of this 30-acre park is the three-story field house designed and constructed in 1929 by architect Clarence Hatzfeld. The Chicago River streams through the center of the park and you'll often find fishermen casting their lines at the North Branch dam. The park district has even conveniently installed steel rod holders.

The newly developed **Ping Tom Memorial Park** (300 West 19th Street, no phone) is a thoughtfully planned space, with its Asian-influenced plazas set along the southern branch of the Chicago River. It has become the crown jewel of Chicago's Chinatown neighborhood.

For information on the entire Chicago Park District, call 312-742-7529.

S E C R E T
PERIODICALS

It's a no-brainer to say that one surefire way to quickly put your finger on the pulse of any city is by hunkering down with a copy of the local alternative weekly newspaper. Most of the time, these periodicals are free and easy to locate, as they're distributed from colorful, street-corner newspaper boxes. Chicago has several free alt weeklies. I'm a bit biased in this category, though. As a contributor and staff writer for *New City* for three years, I must side with this little tabloid spitfire. Publishers (and husband-and-wife team) Brian and Jan Hieggelke started *New City* in 1984, putting it together in their living room. Today, the paper has 150,000 weekly readers and the Heiggelkes have put up a snappy Web site (www.newcitynet.com), which brings together the crème de la crème of stories from alternative weeklies across the nation. Although the editorial content of *New City* has a more street-savvy voice than any of the competition's, I must admit that the paper may not be the most complete source for listings. But, if you want to get in touch with what's really cool in

Chicago, there's no better outlet. *New City* has comprehensive club listings and its coverage of the literary community is unparalleled in Chicago. It comes out every Wednesday, in bright orange newspaper boxes all across the city and suburbs.

The ***Chicago Reader***, on the other hand, is a monstrous paper. It's available each Thursday, mostly inside bookstores, music shops, and retail establishments, as well as in yellow street-corner boxes. The going joke in Chicago is that no one actually "reads" the *Reader*. The cover stories go nose-to-nose with Tolstoy in length and, even worse, they often make for good sleep aids. This said, the *Reader* is the single best place to find listings for plays, movies, concerts, and other events in and around the Chicagoland area.

*UR **Chicago*** is a fledgling operation, produced monthly, with a strong focus on the collegiate crowd. The paper is free and can be found in coffee shops, trendy record shops, bookstores, and other hipster havens. Because it comes out only once a month, timeliness is a bit of an issue, but since appearing in 1997, this paper has improved by leaps and bounds.

Chicago's large gay population has two comprehensive publications to turn to: ***Windy City Times***, which has some of the best photojournalism spreads of any newspaper, and the newsmagazine ***Gay Chicago***, now more than 22 years old, which has very comprehensive theater and restaurant reviews.

Of course, you can always turn to the weekend sections of the ***Chicago Tribune*** and the ***Chicago Sun-Times***. Both papers boast strong coverage of music, theater, films, and restaurants. The *Tribune* also has an offspring Web site, **Metromix** (www.metromix.com), which, in my opinion, is the very best source for reviews. The monster database covers everything from art galleries and storefront theater to hamburger joints.

SECRET
PHOTOGRAPHY

I'm not much for the art-fart gallery openings where the wine and cheese and all the posturing are more important than the creativity on the walls. There are several wonderful photography galleries in Chicago, however, where all the pretension is left at the door.

The **Museum of Contemporary Photography** (600 South Michigan Avenue, 312-663-5554) is the city's preeminent museum dedicated completely to photography and nothing but photography. It occupies a large space in the main building of Columbia College, a local arts and communications school. The exhibits rotate regularly, every two months or so, and showcase striking contemporary work from 1959 to the present. Recent shows have included a 50-year retrospective of celebrity photographer Victor Skrebneski, a showcase of Midwest photographers, and the work of Ansel Adams. The shows here are always outstanding, and always equally concerned with social issues and photographic technique.

Smack dab in the middle of Chicago's snooty River North art gallery district is a true anomaly. **Stephen Daiter** (311 West Superior Street, Suite 404, 312-787-3350) is accessible and, despite the neighbors, still full of that grassroots creativity that makes for fabulous art. It is also one of the best photo galleries in Chicago. You'll find vintage and modern photography here, along with shelves of books and comfy chairs to encourage conversation with strangers. The collection of 20th-century documentary and experimental work, including Bauhaus and Photo League, is splendid. A recent showing of both past and present photographs from *The New York Times* photo archives was a winner. This is a special place with a knowledgeable and kind staff.

When tourists swarm into the **Art Institute of Chicago** (111 South Michigan Avenue, 312-443-3600), they usually make a beeline straight up the marble staircase to the second floor toward the cache of Monet paintings. And really, you can't blame them. These paintings are beautiful. But what a lot of people don't realize is that the museum has a stunning collection of photographs on display in the basement. Just once, go downstairs and look. You won't regret it.

Yet another wonderful, long-standing, and still very much accessible gallery is **Artemisia** (700 North Carpenter Street, 312-226-7323). The emphasis here is on the role of women in the arts, focusing particularly on experimental work that would be shunned by the snobby commercial houses. The cause is good and the art is better.

S E C R E T
PICASSO

The last time I was at the **Art Institute of Chicago** (111 South Michigan Avenue, 312-443-3600), a friend of mine guided me through the museum to show me a little-known secret hidden within the classic oil painting *Old Guitarist*, by Pablo Picasso.

First, you have to understand my friend. Michael Hart is one of this country's great visionaries. Back in 1971, he told the world that this thing called the Internet would be a repository for cool information — an Alexandria Library for the digital age. The 100 or so Department of Defense creeps and university nerds who were online thought Hart was nuts. They were wrong. From the cluttered basement of his downstate Illinois home, he now runs **Project Gutenberg** (www.

gutenberg.net), the première place to download public domain literary works in their entirety. We're talking Shakespeare, Melville, Twain, the Human Genome Project, and another 4,000 works and counting. And you thought Napster was cool. Michael can see things most people do not.

And that brings us back to Picasso. Ever heard of a "magic-eye" picture? They're those dotted drawings that so many people were talking about a few years back. If you stared at them straight on, you just saw a series of colored dots. That was it. But if you let your vision blur, three-dimensional images would jump out at you. Dinosaurs and sharks and things. I could never find any of it. And I always felt like an idiot. So there I am, standing in the whisper-only halls of the Art Institute, when Michael tells me about the hidden woman within *Old Guitarist.* I'm thinking, "Oh shit, magic eye." So I stared at the beautiful, melancholy painting for a good long time, looking real hard and seeing nothing but what I was supposed to: the old guitarist. But then, suddenly, there she was. The faint, apparitional image of the woman looming just behind the central figure in the painting. While some dispute her presence, at least to me, she is visually unavoidable. And very beautiful. As my friend explained, for those who believe in the woman's presence, the meaning of this melancholy painting is that the sorrowful man is playing a sad tune on his guitar after his pregnant wife died while giving birth. To coin a phrase: believe it, or not.

S E C R E T
PIZZA

While this book is dedicated to all the little off-the-beaten-path places in and around the Windy City, we'd be doing you a complete disservice by simply ignoring the popular, tourist-trap pizzerias just because they're no longer a secret. So here they are, in one quick pitch. Siblings **Pizzeria Uno** (29 East Ohio Street, 312-321-1000) and **Pizzeria Due** (619 North Wabash Avenue, 312-943-2400) gave birth to what we now know as the Chicago-style pizza, a deep-dish brick of gooey cheese and piping-hot ingredients smothered within. Situated downtown, these twin establishments are blocks away from one another, so if you can't get into Uno, try Due. Definitely get ready to stand in line at **Gino's East** (160 East Superior Street, 312-943-1124), another favorite deep-dish Mecca. While it takes a good 30 to 45 minutes to cook one of these babies, part of the fun is adding to the graffiti art already established on the walls. For years, people have been writing all over the walls, the ceiling, the restroom stalls, the chairs, and just about anywhere else.

One more great pie to behold is at **Giordano's**, with 39 locations in the city and suburbs. Here are just a few of my favorites. If you're shopping on the Magnificent Mile, stop off at 730 North Rush Street (312-951-0747). While wandering the halls of the Art Institute, you can work up a ferocious appetite — luckily, there's a pizza nearby, in the basement of 28 East Jackson (312-939-4646). After a show at one of the many fabulous storefront theaters on the North Side of town, I have often paid a late-night visit to 1040 West Belmont Avenue (773-327-1200). I've taken many out-of-town friends to Giordano's and they've never left disappointed. And the consensus is that the deep-dish spinach is the best.

Now, let's talk places the locals try to keep all to themselves. Try not to tell too many people about these places, okay? For four years, I lived next to a family of true Chicagoans. The men drank beer for breakfast. They watched Bears games on a tiny TV in their backyard on Sundays. They played darts in their garage until the wee hours of the night. These great friends, lifelong Chicagoans, let me in on their pizza secret. The **Chicago Pizza and Oven Grinder Company** (2121 North Clark Street, 773-248-2570) serves up the most incredible little individual pizza potpies. They come out upside down, and the waiters throw a plate on top of the mound, flip the thing over, and tap out the mushroom-like pizza concoction. There are two sizes — one pound and half pound — both baked brown, loaded with a delightful red sauce, melting cheese, and your choice of ingredients. And try the Mediterranean bread and the salad with poppy seed dressing. Be prepared to wait, though. Longtime Chicago residents know about this place and the lines on weekends can extend out the door with an hour of waiting time.

A completely different experience is waiting for you at **Marie's Pizza, Dining Room and Lounge** (4127 West Lawrence Avenue, 773-725-1812). As you enter through the liquor store at the front of this neighborhood pizzeria, you'll find the waitresses still have bouffant hairdos and chew gum while they take your order. Except this is no theme restaurant routine, this is the real McCoy. The thin-crust pizza is mighty tasty, but this place is more about atmosphere than food.

White Sox fans swear by **Home Run Inn** (4254 West 31st Street, 773-247-9696), a 78-year-old pizzeria that's off the radar of most tourists. The neighborhood is old-time Chicago and, as legend has it, the name of the restaurant itself dates back to the 1920s, when it was just a tavern. As the story goes, a winning run from a local little-league baseball game came crashing through the front window. Today, the place is legendary with locals. The pizza, both thin and thick crust, isn't just a home run, it's a damned grand slam.

Chicago movie critic Roger Ebert once called **Pat's Pizza** (3114 North Sheffield Avenue, 773-880-6506) the tops in the city for thin crust. Whether it's the best or not, it definitely gets an enthusiastic "thumbs up." Try the house special, appropriately named "The Pat's," which features sausage, mushrooms, onion, and green peppers. Another *really* good thin-crust pie is served at **D'Agostino's Pizzeria** (1351 West Addison Street, 773-477-1821). This no-frills pizza pub, which opened in 1968, is a dark, red-and-white tablecloth, neighborhood kind of joint. The secret to the pizza is twofold: wafer-thin, crispy crust and super sweet tomato sauce.

For late-night munchies, **Chicago's Pizza** (3006 North Sheffield Avenue, 773-477-2777; 1742 West Wilson Avenue, 773-506-8888) delivers until 5 AM. They go heavy on the garlic and tomato sauce. Other specialties: the Grecian Delight with goat cheese, green olives, sun-dried tomatoes, roasted red peppers, mozzarella cheese, and sliced fresh tomatoes in pesto sauce. Be daring and try the Bar-B-Que with grilled, marinated chicken, red onions, fresh cilantro, smoked gouda, and mozzarella.

SECRET
POLICE

The oft-maligned Chicago Police Department tries to put a positive spin on all those old allegations of corruption and impropriety at the

American Police Center Museum (1717 South State Street, 312-431-0005). After the inner-city and antiwar riots of the late '60s, and the police beatings in Grant Park during the 1968 Democratic National Convention, the CPD opened this museum in 1974 to polish its image. This museum proves that Chicago's finest have more often than not upheld their pledge to "serve and protect." One hundred years of cops and crooks are captured in countless photographs, uniforms, badges, and weapons. There's also a moving display of those officers who have died in the line of duty. Now, if only the CPD would quit giving me parking tickets.

If you would like to learn more about the underbelly of Chicago's boys in blue, however, local author **Richard Lindberg** has penned a fascinating book, *To Serve and Collect* (Southern Illinois University Press). In fact, history buffs will want to check out the entirety of the Lindberg canon, 11 books in total, all on Chi-town. From the meticulous baseball book *The White Sox Encyclopedia* (Temple University Press) to the fascinating *Chicago by Gaslight: A History of Chicago's Netherworld, 1880–1920* (Academy Chicago Publishers), he is an expert on all things Chicago.

The more than 13,000 uniformed police officers in Chicago get some pretty snazzy black leather jackets come wintertime. The coats are super heavy, fully lined, and proudly display the CPD patch on the sleeve. You can buy an authentic used Chicago Police jacket at **The Alley** (858 West Belmont Avenue, 773-883-1800), a clothing store that is a part of the **Alternative Shopping Complex** (858 West Belmont Avenue, 773-348-5000). This entire five-store Mecca (which includes clothing, a gothic plaster-sculpture shop, a cigar store, a jewelry shop, and a lingerie store) is a magnet for pseudo punk-rock high school kids who come to hang around, smoke cigarettes, and buy some spray-on hair dye that washes out before mommy and daddy can ever see it. Remember when you had to dye your hair for real? Still, The Alley does carry a humongous selection of cool T-shirts and the aforementioned cop coats. Sorry, the CPD patches on the sleeves have been intentionally defaced for legal purposes.

Want to play cops and robbers on an adult scale? **Chicago Motors** (2553 West Chicago Avenue, 773-235-6500) is the Midwest's largest dealer of used police cars — 60 to 185 on the lot at any given time. Ford Crown Victorias. Chevy Caprices. From police departments around the country. And they're built to be abused. They come equipped with big tires, super-strong suspensions, and engines on steroids. These are muscle cars. Most of them have odometer readings of 70,000 to 80,000 miles, and they sell from as low as $1,000 to as high as $9,000. Who buys these prowlers? Mostly cab and security companies, but an individual strolls in about twice a week.

SECRET
POLYNESIAN

Next to Chicago, I love Hawaii. If you've never been, put it on your "to do" list. Sure, it's been pillaged by developers, but there are areas of the islands that are still, well, a secret. But that's another book. What I love is the cheesy, Las Vegas aspect of the islands: hula skirts and floral leis, Elvis performing "Blue Hawaii," and, of course, tikis. Chicago is an unlikely place to find a slice of South Seas exotica, yet it's here.

At the **Hala Kahiki** (2834 North River Road, River Grove, 708-456-3222), the old urban legend of a waitress accidentally lighting herself on fire when delivering one of those flaming, tropical cocktails is absolutely true. Today, the staff is forbidden to wear polyester Hawaiian shirts as a result. You will discover this palace of tropical kitsch in suburban River Grove, just 20 minutes west of downtown Chicago. From the alluring jungle rhythms of vibraphones and bongos to the 20-page tropical drink menu, this place is all about the booze. You won't find Hawaiian pupus on this menu. In fact, there's no food at all. You'd better eat something before visiting this reasonably priced tiki hut. One too many volcanoes or mai tais and you'll be kneeling to the Hawaiian bathroom god.

Trader Vic's (17 East Monroe Street, 312-917-7317), while a little on the expensive side, gets high marks for décor. This Polynesian paradise in the basement of the Palmer House Hotel is decked out like a thatched-hut village on a remote island. From floor to ceiling, the fish netting, the bamboo, and the coconut shells lend themselves to the perfect happy-hour luau. At lunchtime, the Chinese buffet is well stocked, but it's late at night when this place really comes alive with the dark and mysterious allure of the islands. Try a fog cutter or the world-famous mai tai, concocted with two rums and freshly squeezed lime juice.

These drinks are terrific, but it's on Chicago's South Side that you will find the true Polynesian hidden treasure. It is called the Tiki Zombie. Made from a 1,000-year-old tropical recipe, this tall rum libation packs such a wallop, the management of the **House of Tiki** (1612 East 53rd Street, 773-684-1221) allows only one per customer. This is a late-night Chicago bar, where the people are already sauced when they walk in the door. Once you visit this place — decorated with conch shells, beaded curtains, and wooden warrior masks — you'll be saying "Aloha" again and again.

SECRET
POOL

There aren't many left. *Real* pool halls. The kind with ceiling fans thumping rhythmically over pristine green felt tables. The kind where late-afternoon sunlight falls in through slatted windows, carrying with it dancing golden particles of dust. The kind with old metal lockers and even older men sitting stone faced in corners, cues in hand. At the height of pool's popularity in the roaring '20s, some historians of the game have ventured to guess, Cook County (of which Chicago is a part) had more than 5,000 licensed halls. I asked my good buddy Keir, an avid pool man, to give me a little history of the game in Chicago. As Keir explained, in the early 1930s, pool king Willie Mosconi could outdraw the Bears and, from 1948 to 1951, he defended the world championship in a specially constructed arena on Navy Pier. Today, pool halls have dwindled in number to a rare few. Somewhat paradoxically, the Billiard Congress of America figures that nearly 40 million Americans enjoy the sport. So why are pool halls on the endangered species list? We're not sure. But they are out there. Why don't you join us? We'll rack.

First stop on our pool tour is **Chris's Billiards** (4637 North Milwaukee Avenue, 773-286-4714). Located on the second floor of a building on Chicago's Northwest Side, with 49 tables, this is as close as you're going to get to that classic pool hall vibe. Phony wood paneling. Old, dank carpeting. Thick smoke hovering in the air. Very serious players. And the best thing — it's open daily until 2 AM.

The **Chicago Billiard Café** (5935 West Irving Park Road, 773-545-5102), which opened its doors in 1985, has 17 tables and is another favorite spot with serious players of the game. It's also in an old part of town where the Chicago accents are thick and where ice-cold beer on tap is the breakfast of champions. **Marie's Golden Cue** (3241 West Montrose Avenue, 773-478-2555) is another real pool hall, with 19 tables and cue lockers to boot.

SECRET
PORN

Porn addicts take comfort — there are several places in Chicago to satiate your most prurient desires. **Over 21 Bookstore** (1347 North Wells Street, 312-337-8730) is open 24 hours and is well stocked with hardcore and soft-porn magazines, books, and videos. This little shop is in the heart of Old Town, one of the city's ritziest districts. Next door is a Chicago porno institution, the **Bijou Theater** (1349 North Wells Street, 312-943-5397), open 24 hours, seven days a week. It screens gay porn and also stocks more than 5,000 videos for sale. Interested in cruising? It's a happening spot.

Another 24-hour-a-day adult bookstore is **Adult Fantasy** (2928 North Broadway Street, 773-525-9705). Here, you'll find more of those nasty shrink-wrapped "three for $6.99" magazine deals. You might also want to try **Erotic Warehouse** (1246 West Randolph Street, 312-226-5222), yet another 24-hour sex wonderland. If you're a businessperson in town for a convention and need a quick fix, pay a call on **Wells Books** (178 North Wells Street, 312-263-9266). This adult magazine and bookstore carries more than 700 magazines, 2,400 videos, and more than 500 DVDs. According to those who run the operation, the best-selling title is *Hustler XXX*, Larry Flynt's hardcore version of his long-running publication.

S E C R E T
RESTROOMS

As the old saying goes, "When you gotta go, you gotta go." But sometimes, locating a public restroom for quick relief is out of the question. Even a spokesperson for Mayor Richard M. Daley's office confirms the worst — there just aren't many public restrooms to be found, particularly downtown. And once you do locate a city-sanctioned latrine, it becomes apparent that the mayor's citywide beautification program hasn't spread to the public restrooms. Tread carefully when entering. But, beyond dropping trow in an alleyway, there are alternatives. Many of the city's most opulent hotels have some absolutely palatial pissers, replete with marble floors, shoeshines, and pricey bar-soap. And best of all, these washrooms are, in most cases, located right in the lobby. Good johns include the **Chicago Hilton Hotel and Towers** (720 South Michigan Avenue, 312-922-4400), the **Palmer House** (17 East Monroe Street, 312-782-8258), the **Four Seasons** (120 East Delaware Place, 312-280-8800), and the **Hyatt** (151 East Wacker Drive, 312-565-1234). Just act like you belong in the lobby, walk confidently, and blend in with the clientele.

Many retail and department stores have restrooms, including Marshall Field's, Carson's, and Bloomingdale's. On the top floor of **Nike Town** (669 North Michigan Avenue, 312-642-6363) on the Magnificent Mile, there are some nice restrooms with Nike's trademark "swoosh" logo serving as the door handles. The **Harold Washington Public Library** (400 South State Street, 312-747-4300) has restrooms on each of its nine floors; the closest is on the second floor. The **Virgin Megastore** (540 North Michigan Avenue, 312-645-9300) also has restrooms on the second level. I myself champion the restrooms in the **House of Blues** (329 North Dearborn Street, 312-527-2583). They're so clean you could eat off the floor, and there's even a powder room with a shoeshine man, ritzy cologne, and a big tankard of minty-fresh mouthwash.

Believe it or not, right next to Buckingham Fountain, there is a suitable **public restroom** that is relatively well maintained and, unlike the street-side johns in San Francisco, free of charge. I wouldn't necessarily recommend sitting down, but still, in a pinch, it'll do.

Finally, all the numerous bookstores like Barnes and Noble have "public" restrooms. But the Borders store at Clark and Diversey just may spoil these easy-access restrooms. In 1998, in an effort to curtail vagrants, the store installed locks on the door, requiring customers to get tokens from the sales counter. Spoilsports.

SECRET
RICK KOGAN

No writer alive today understands the concrete, iron, and rust fabric of the Windy City better than *Chicago Tribune* staffer Rick Kogan. For 30 years, Kogan has covered the streets of this rough yet gentle city. From the icy spray of Lake Michigan waves in January to the spring tulips of Grant Park, Kogan knows Chicago and he writes about it with affection. With every word in print that bears his byline, you just hear his love of Chicago coming through in his gravelly barroom voice. So I asked Rick Kogan to name a few of his own favorite secret places in Chicago. Lean closer, pour yourself a stiff drink, if you're so inclined, and listen closely. This man knows Chicago.

"**Lincoln Tavern** (1858 West Wabansia Avenue, 773-342-7778) is a vital member of that vanishing urban species known as the family-run neighborhood saloon, with an adjoining dining room with a homemade feel, in both the menu and north woods decor.

"**City Newsstand** (4018 North Cicero Avenue, 773-545-7377) is a place to find the Sunday papers from Prague, Paris, China, and 50 places in between, as well as more than 600 magazine titles.

"**Buzz Café** (905 South Lombard Avenue, Oak Park, 708-524-2899) is a coffee shop/gallery/restaurant/performance space run by a former *Tribune* graphics wiz. According to me and Poetry Slam founder Marc Smith, it's the hippest place in the western suburbs.

"**Mario's Italian Lemonade** (1066 West Taylor Street, no phone, see "Secret Italian Ice") is a one-story wooden shack painted a happy white and red and offering the best Italian lemonade (in flavors galore) to a crowd that is a wonderful mix and mixes wonderfully, as if they are all visiting a religious shrine.

"**Prairie Joe's** (1921 Central Street, Evanston, 847-491-0391) is a study in comfortable informality, with all manner of vintage 'junk' — cameras, salt and pepper shakers, record albums, stereos, artwork — and great, inventive food.

"**Royko Grove** (at Montrose Point in Lincoln Park, Montrose Avenue at Lake Michigan) — named for legendary Chicago newspaperman Mike Royko, and marked by small trees planted by Mike's pals after his death in 1997 — is a serene place that has the best view of the city available from the North Side.

"**Iron Mike's Grille** (100 East Chestnut Street, 312-587-8989), a shrine to former Bears player and coach Mike Ditka, is also a very good steak joint. It's a place for people with large appetites and thirsts."

S E C R E T
ROCK

❧

If you like to rock, you've come to the right place. Chicago has a killer scene. National acts play multiple nights in the city's cavernous arenas. And big-name bands sometimes pop up, unannounced, in small clubs. You'll find 2,500-seat theaters with perfect sight lines and perfect sound, and historic old ballrooms where the atmosphere and energy are as voltaic as the crunch of a power chord on a Les Paul guitar. You'll find raw clubs where the floor is slicked with beer and the elevated train screeches by outside on frigid winter nights. Best of all, you'll find any kind of rock that rocks your world. On any night of the week, you can ferret out power-pop and punk, metal and ska, glam and roots. Yes indeed, Chicago likes to rock. For listings, consult *New City* or the *Chicago Reader* (see "Secret Periodicals").

Over the years as an alternative newspaper writer, I've had the good fortune to interview tons of really cool bands. And when my tape recorder stops running and I put my pad and pen away, I always ask, just out of curiosity, what their favorite venues are in the country. The reason I ask is that many of them name the same place. For instance, the **Metro** (3730 North Clark Street, 773-549-0203) pops up quite a bit. This house, with a capacity of 1,100, is really just an old theater with the floor seats ripped out. If you want to jam, stay on the floor where, depending on the ferociousness of the band on stage, a mosh pit is likely to ensue. But be careful, though. If you get hoisted in the air, watch your fall. The floor is A-1, rock-solid concrete and it hurts. Bad. But don't get scared off. It's not always rowdy in here and you can retreat up to the second-floor balcony, where the view of the stage is stellar and the sound comes together in one loud, crystalline punch. Did I mention it was loud? Lots of local artists earned their stripes at the Metro: Smashing Pumpkins, Ministry, Liz Phair. And lots of huge bands forgo the big venues and play here because they love it. Like Cheap Trick, Slayer, and, even now that they're platinum empowered, the Pumpkins. This is simply the best place in Chicago to see a band.

The exterior of **Double Door** (1572 North Milwaukee Avenue, 773-489-3160) is a movie casting director's dream. Right under the elevated train track that eventually ends at O'Hare International Airport, on a busy, gritty six-corner intersection, this popular rock venue is in the heart of Wicker Park — the city's bohemian, artsy alcove. Keyword here: diversity. With its schizo booking policy, you're liable to see all sorts of bands blasting all sorts of sounds. One night you'll hear industrial, the next you'll be jamming to punkabilly. A few years back, the Rolling Stones even played an unannounced full set here as a tour warmup. This is rock 'n' roll. After a two-hour sweat-fest, you'll leave with your ears ringing, your hair smelling of cigs, and your bladder ready to burst. There are only two johns in this place and they're about the size of a practice amplifier.

Yet another really cool, way off-the-trodden-trail club is the **Hideout** (1354 West Wabansia Avenue, 773-227-4433). Sandwiched into a rusty industrial corridor, this venue is tops when it comes to country and roots rock.

For rockabilly diehards, look no further than **The California Clipper** (1002 North California Avenue, 773-384-2547). While the atmosphere feels like a 1920s speakeasy, the crowd is all about pompadours, tattoos, cuffed blue jeans, and hot rods. Every Wednesday night there's live rockabilly but even without the tunes, this is a bad-ass bar. The weekend lineup of live music is excellent too.

For those in-between bands that can't quite pack a stadium but don't want to play a club, the **Aragon Ballroom** (1106 West Lawrence Avenue) is the answer. This 5,000-seat palace used to host the big bands of the 1940s. Back then, playing the Aragon meant you had "arrived." Everyone from Frank Sinatra and Tommy Dorsey to Glenn Miller was booked here. Standing outside and looking up at this grand old monster, you can envision the time when it was an opulent house for musical events. Today, it attracts punk and rock and metal acts and just reeks of stale beer. In fact, up until a few years ago, they served the beer in jumbo movie-popcorn buckets. Mid-show, when the beer was gone, the buckets turned into handy-dandy-I-won't-miss-a-note-urinals. If you want to find out who's playing the Aragon (affectionately known to locals as the "Scaragon" or the "Brawlroom"), call **Ticketmaster** at 312-559-1212.

Here are some other top clubs for local rock bands. The **Empty Bottle** (1035 North Western Avenue, 773-276-3600) is always jam-packed and always rocking. It's easy to miss though; the sign is small, so you're gonna have to trust me on this one. For Chicagoans who really love the music scene, this is one of the top spots. Join their e-mail list to find out about upcoming events at www.emptybottle.com. **Fireside Bowl** (2646 West Fullerton Avenue, 773-486-2700) is a hardcore punk rock paradise in an old bowling alley. By the way, you can still bowl here on occasion. It's $2 per game and $1 for shoes.

SECRET
ROMANTIC RESTAURANTS

Ever want to head out for a quiet, romantic night on the town and you somehow end up in an over-lit, hectic restaurant where the waiters are running back and forth, dishes are clanking in the kitchen, the phone is ringing, busboys bump you, and your table is four packs of sugar shy of level? I feel your pain. And fortunately, I have romance-ready solutions.

If the apple of your eye asks "How 'bout Italian?" my suggestion is **Angelina Ristorante** (3561 North Broadway Street, 773-935-5933), a dark and intimate trattoria. It's low key with the requisite candlelit tables. **A Tavola** (2152 West Chicago Avenue, 773-276-7567), located in the Ukrainian Village neighborhood, is another quiet, romantic Italian secret. Do not miss the gnocchi prepared in brown butter and sage sauce. The service is professional and well paced.

At **Geja's** (340 West Armitage Avenue, 773-281-9101) the walls of wine bottles reflect the dim light, and couples stare longingly into each other's . . . fondue. This Lincoln Park restaurant has been a favorite with lovers for a long time. Where else will you see people dipping generous chunks of bread and hand feeding their partners?

Speaking of bread, if you adhere to the "you can't have romance without finance" theory, then by all means take the amazingly fast elevator ride to the **Signature Room** (875 North Michigan Avenue, 312-787-9596) on the 95th floor of the John Hancock Center. Here, you can dine on roasted Colorado lamb chops with whipped potatoes

and turnips in a red wine shallot sauce for 30 bucks. And a little perk? You'll have the best view of downtown Chicago in the entire city.

Looking for something artsy, something snug as a bug, something special? Oh baby, venture no further than **Lula's Café** (2537 North Kedzie Avenue, 773-489-9554). The space, adorned by colorful artwork and strung with twinkle lights, only holds about 50 people. The eclectic, multi-ethnic menu changes regularly but includes all sorts of inexpensive, fusion-inspired entrées. The pasta dishes and the vegetarian sesame maki rolls come mightily recommended. But the real joy here is the cozy, bohemian charm.

For something completely different, understated, and low key, grab a sidewalk table on a summer evening at **El Tinajon** (2054 West Roscoe Street, 773-525-8455). This is an authentic Guatemalan eatery, radiating a warm and festive atmosphere and serving Guatemalan versions of familiar favorites like tacos, tamales, and enchiladas. The plantains here come recommended, along with the spicy black beans and the sizable margaritas in fruity flavors of peach and mango and banana.

SECRET

SAGANAKI

If you have never been to Greek Town, let me set the scene. The better restaurants in this district (Halsted Street, from Madison Street to Van Buren Street) are dark and candlelit. Just as you polish off one jug of velvety red wine, another appears. You talk and you laugh and you drink. And then everything suddenly halts when the waiter comes with a tray and cries "Opaaa!" as he splashes brandy and lemon over a slice of broiled kefalograviera cheese, and lights it on fire. This is saganaki, or flaming Greek cheese. The folks at the **Parthenon** (314 South Halsted Street, 312-726-2407) boast that they invented this Chicago Greek Town original back in 1968. And this might well be true — after all, they do this appetizer better than almost anyone. Almost. While the differences are subtle, the saganaki at **Greek Islands** (200 South Halsted Street, 312-782-9855) is fried a perfect golden brown on the outside, with piping-hot cheese inside. And there's that ever-so slight hint of lemon juice, just tart enough to make your taste buds wince for a moment. But then you go back for seconds.

And when it's time to venture beyond saganaki, the winner for the overall best Greek restaurant, in case you were wondering, is **Santorini** (800 West Adams Street, 312-829-8820). This busy, noisy restaurant does more than others with its menu (especially the seafood) and with its décor, a warm, Mediterranean isle setting. Here, you'll get your delectable wedge of lemon-spritzed flaming cheese and oh so much more. Try the perfectly grilled octopus. Tantalizing entrées include the swordfish kabob, an impressive skewer of chunky filets, blackened peppers, and onions, and the black sea bass in a lovely lemon butter sauce.

SECRET
SANDWICHES

Capt'n Nemo's (3650 North Ashland Avenue, 773-929-7687) is a well-kept secret with Cubs fans, who park their cars a few blocks from Wrigley Field and walk to the ball game. Along the way, they stop at this cheap fast food joint for a submarine sandwich or an Italian sausage sandwich loaded up with peppers and onions and tomato sauce. But the real secrets here (especially in the cold winter months) are the daily soup specials. My favorite: split pea. Cap'n Nemo's also has a second location (7367 North Clark Street, 773-973-0570).

A popular sandwich shop with De Paul University students is the **Pot Belly Sandwich Works** (2264 North Lincoln Avenue, 773-528-1405). For $3.83, you can buy what most in the neighborhood call the best submarine sandwich in town. Popular choices include the Italian and the ham and Swiss. For vegetarians, the sandwich makers build a monster veggie sandwich. And for travelers, the shop recently added a location in the new Midway Airport terminal.

Costello's Sandwich & Sides (2015 West Roscoe Street, 773-929-2323) is an old-fashioned sandwich shop. It's hunkered into a cozy grouping of stores and restaurants on a tree-lined street that feels like classic Main Street, USA. In the summer, the shop puts a few tables out on the sidewalk, and there's always a crowd for lunch. But even with a line at the counter, the oven-baked sannys and hot soups are worth the wait.

SECRET
SHORTCUTS

As the old saying goes, in Chicago, there are two seasons — winter and construction. And while I don't want to bemoan the state of our fair city, there is some measure of truth in this statement. Each

spring, when the birds start chirpin' and the leaves start poppin', burly men in orange hard hats get asphalt choppin'. While the official colors on the Chicago flag are blue and white, the real colors may as well be road worker orange. Sometimes, midsummer, with all the street construction, when the mercury on the thermometer is ready to boil over, Chicago looks like war-torn Baghdad. But you can find ways around the endless barrage of detours, lane closures, and expressway migraines. Follow me.

Elston Avenue is a great alternative to the Kennedy Expressway. Running from the far Northwest Side all the way south to the fringe of downtown, Elston can get you there in a hurry when the traffic is bad. And the best part about Elston Avenue is that, when you reach the southern end, you are within spitting distance of the **Matchbox** (770 North Milwaukee Avenue, 312-666-9292), a great tavern that, as the name implies, is just a little sliver of a watering hole. At its skinniest, this tavern is just three feet wide. Lettering on one of the street-side windows even calls it "Chicago's most intimate bar." Since it has a width as narrow as a yardstick, how can you dispute the claim? On a Friday evening after work, be careful — you're in danger of getting crushed. And try the vodka gimlets — they are the best the city has to offer.

When Chicago's boys in orange are out shredding asphalt, getting back and forth to Midway Airport via the Stevenson Expressway is enough to make anyone want to go postal. But fret not, weary traveler: **Archer Avenue** is at your disposal. This street can take you to Midway, lickety split. You'll bypass the Stevenson gridlock and you will see a true slice of working-class Chicago along the way.

Bogged down in traffic on the city's North Side? Trying to traverse Ashland, Damen, or Western and it's a preview of hell? Look for Ravenswood Avenue, a predominantly quiet, industrial street that runs north and south. There are few stoplights, mostly stop signs, and in gridlock this can be a helpful alternative.

SECRET
SKYLINE

Get your camera out and make sure the film is loaded. Here is a list of the best places to view Chicago's world-renowned skyline. And while you're admiring the view, remember that it is because of the wisdom of Chicago's forefathers that the lakefront is unobstructed. While an 1836 doctrine called for the lakefront to remain "forever open, clear and free," for years greedy developers clamored for this valuable land. Retail tycoon Aaron Montgomery Ward came to Chicago's rescue. Between 1890 and 1922, Ward sued the city four times to keep it from developing the land. Then, in 1909, architect and city planner Daniel Burnham presented his Plan for Chicago, an urban blueprint outlining his future vision of the city. Within this doctrine Burnham called for a system of parks, a system of super-highways, and an unobstructed lakefront. Today, 29 miles of lakefront shoreline is undeveloped and open to the public. And all this wonderful open space provides dramatic vantage points of the skyline to end all skylines.

At the very end of the **Adler Planetarium** peninsula (1300 South Lake Shore Drive, 312-322-0300), you will find a postcard-perfect view of the city. Another vantage point that people always seem to ooh and ahh about is on **North Avenue Beach** (North Avenue and the lake). Walk past the park district building that looks like a ship

and venture out onto one of the concrete piers. You'll get a great shot of the John Hancock Center, and Navy Pier and its Ferris wheel. Of course, if you're lazy, you could just buy these shots on a postcard.

Standing in the middle of the **Michigan Avenue Bridge** (400 North Michigan Avenue) is always spectacular. Below you, the Chicago River. All around you, the Tribune Tower, the Wrigley Building, and, out to the east, Lake Michigan.

SECRET
SMELT

Every year between March 1 and April 30, the smelters come out at night. Smelt fishing is an annual rite of passage in Chicago. The best place to catch them is at **Montrose Harbor** (4600 North Lake Shore), where teams of families gather on the lakeshore to build fires and fish with nets for the little silvery buggers that are not much bigger than a minnow. As smelt legend has it, sometime around 1913, some wiseacre had the bright idea to import these two-to-three-inch fish from their native waters in the Atlantic Ocean to Lake Crystal in Michigan. Eventually, as the story goes, a few of the fish migrated into the Great Lakes and the rest, as they say, is "fishstory." But you don't have to be a fisherman — or even like to eat fish, for that matter — to enjoy the spectacle of the short-lived smelt season. Come on out, have a beer or two from a friendly fisherman's ice chest, and, if you're brave enough, have him fry you up a bunch. And, oh yes, the best way to locate the smelt fishermen is by the lights of their fires. Don't be shy — they're a nice lot of people.

If you don't want to go through the effort of freezing your buns off on the shores of Lake Michigan (it's almost always cold out there at this time of year), you can pick up a pound of fried smelt for just $4.49 at **Hagen's Fish Market** (5835 West Montrose Avenue, 773-283-1944). This 57-year-old business is owned by Don Breede, a son-in-law of the original owners. Ask Don about any fish and he's likely to give you a great education. This kind of place is what Chicago is all about — blue collar, friendly, and down to earth.

SECRET
SPANKING

We all have our naughty little secrets now, don't we? If getting or giving a good swat in the ass is your thing, the **Leather Rose** (2537 West Fullerton Avenue, 773-276-6090) is your best and most discreet bet. You wouldn't know this devilish establishment existed if you were just passing by. The undistinguished storefront bears no signage. This is strictly a word-of-mouth business. So just walk through the front door. You'll enter a sadomasochist's lair of whips and cuffs and paddles and floggers. The s-m shop caters to a multitude of deviant desires. There are blindfolds and — ahem — ball stretchers and masks, leather leashes and riding crops and harnesses, and, when you're feeling the *amore*, leather roses. But that's not all. Enter the back room and you come upon a hush-hush world of dark debauchery. On any given night you'll find men in drag, tied to the wall, getting feather-tickled by their ladies. On the floor, in the middle of this dank den, couples copulate in front of imperturbable onlookers. And while there's a bar, they don't serve booze. The proprietors of this upstanding establishment don't want patrons to lose control on a bad beer buzz.

S E C R E T

SPICE

❧

I *love* spicy food. In fact, I like it so hot, that a lot of people ask if I can even taste the food behind all the cayenne, jalapeno, or, best and hottest of them all, habanero. You bet. Spices just accentuate the chow to my armor-clad taste buds. But here's the conundrum for all spice extremists: most restaurants say they'll do it up right, and then they come back with the food and it has the kick of a '76 Ford Pinto in the middle of winter with a dead battery. A message to the cooks and chefs of the world — when someone asks for it hot, blaze 'em!

One rainy autumn evening I was in the **Blue Iris Cafe** (3216 North Sheffield Avenue, 773-975-8383), a charming restaurant with delicious Southwestern fare. I ordered the blackened mahi mahi and the waiter asked "How hot do you want it, on a scale of 1 to 10?" Considering my past experiences with restaurants, I replied, "10!" Soon, I watched the chef (in eyeshot of the dining room) start to prepare my meal. Steam was rising from the grill and he was pouring on the seasoning as it rose up and billowed out into the dining room. Within minutes, everyone in the cozy restaurant was coughing. When my meal came out (the one and only time anything has ever been too spicy for my palate) everyone in the restaurant gave me glares of death.

Cajun food has a notorious blast and **Heaven on Seven** (600 North Michigan Avenue, 312-280-7774; 111 North Wabash Avenue, 7th floor, 312-263-6443) serves some of the best Creole cuisine in town. If you like it hot, the "Wall of Fire" is waiting to ignite you. This collection of hot sauces from around the world will spice up your gumbo, po' boy, or red beans and rice.

For Thai food that is amazingly good and can be ordered within a range of spiced-fire, do not — I repeat, *do not* — pass up **Thai Pastry and Restaurant** (4925 North Broadway Street, 773-784-5399). The extensive menu at this outstanding, well-lit eatery includes an array of appetizers, such as the popular fish cakes. For entrées, there is an assortment of noodle, rice, and curry dishes. And don't forget dessert. The Thai custard gets the highest rating possible. Four Forks. Wait, there aren't ratings in this book. Still, you get the point.

S E C R E T

SPOKEN WORD

Almost every night of the week, all over the city, you can unearth open-mic nights, fiction readings, poetry readings, and Chicago's own wacky contribution to verse — poetry slams. What's a poetry slam, you ask? Stop off at the **Green Mill** (4802 North Broadway Street, 773-878-5552) for the **Uptown Poetry Slam** on a Sunday night to discover this Chicago original. The slam began here in the 1980s, a beat-style poetry fest with all the exuberance of a sporting event. It's a grab-bag variety show that mixes together an open stage, special guests, musical and dramatic acts, and lots of rowdy audience interaction. There is a mock competition between poets, scored by judges selected from the crowd. The poetry slam celebrates the performance of poetry as much as the poems themselves, and it's just downright fun. The weekly Uptown event was created by poet Marc Smith 17 years ago. Today, this raucous form of spoken word can be found in more than 150 cities nationwide. But while a good and goofy time is always had by all, the poetry can be powerful, socially aware, and profound. Do visit the Green Mill on Sunday nights. But arrive early (before the 7 PM starting time) — this small, historic bar (see "Secret Jazz") fills up fast and seats are few.

Check out the open mic on Monday nights at the **Funky Buddha Lounge** (728 West Grand Avenue, 312-666-1695) for a cool mix of hip-hop music, verse, and acid jazz. For open-mic poetry, try **Coffee Chicago** (5256 North Broadway Street, 773-784-1305). **Joy Blue** (3998 North Southport Avenue, 773-477-3330) is a friendly neighborhood tavern with Wednesday open-mic nights starting at 9 PM.

Monday and Tuesday nights at **Cafe Aloha** (2156 West Montrose Avenue, 773-907-9356) are fast becoming a hotbed for live bands, performance artists, and open-mic poetry.

Many of the independent bookstores in Chicago host regular author readings (see "Secret Books"). But to discover the next wave of fiction writing talent, contact the **Columbia College Fiction Writing Department** (624 South Michigan Avenue, 312-663-1600, ext. 7615) for a schedule of readings and open-mic events. This is an impressive program, turning out young, cutting-edge authors with bigtime book contracts at Gatling gun velocity. The best bets are the thrice-annual Advanced Fiction Readings, where graduate and undergraduate students read from works in progress. This creative writing program started the Story Workshop Method, now a fixture at colleges and universities across the country. And in the interests of full disclosure — I teach here. Look for me and say hi.

For a dose of spine-tingling spookiness, **Twilight Tales** (Red Lion, 2446 North Lincoln Avenue, 773-348-2695) hosts local horror and science fiction writers on Monday nights. Adding to the flavor, the readings are held in the dark and supposedly haunted room above the wonderful British Red Lion pub (see "Secret Beer Gardens"). Grab a pint of Newcastle and cozy up to a loved one. Some of this stuff would make Stephen King whimper like a baby.

SECRET
STREET FESTS

Every year, nearly 4 million people cram into Grant Park (Randolph Street to Roosevelt Road along Lake Michigan) for the 10-day **Taste of Chicago** festival, held from the end of June through the Fourth of July. Fireworks and a big rock concert in the Petrillo band shell punctuate the end of the fest. Over the years, some great bands have performed, including Cheap Trick, local favorites Poi Dog Pondering, and the great alternative band, the Replacements. But the true allure of the Taste of Chicago is, as the name implies, the food. Local restaurants set up camp to hawk everything from falafel sandwiches, baby back ribs, fried tempura, and roasted quail to slices of ultra deep-dish pizza. During this summer festival, a cloud of wonderful smells drapes over the 304-acre park like a thunderhead. If you happen to be in Chicago at this time, check it out. Once. And then, never come back. Just between us, the prices are steep and the portions usually wouldn't satiate a horsefly. It's crowded, it's sweaty, but still, it's definitely Chicago. Try it and then run like hell.

Now, let's move on to the real "secret" street fests — the little parties held all over the city that fill the streets with laughter, music, games, and food. The **African/Caribbean International Festival of Life,** held at the beginning of July in the Sunken Garden at Washington Park (East 56th Street and South Cottage Grove Avenue), is the true alternative to the Taste of Chicago. Ever had grilled goat? You'll find it here, along with other delectable barbecued morsels, fruit smoothies, and, of course, Caribbean music. This festival also packs in an army of vendors selling African sculpture and carvings, gleaming jewelry, and arts and crafts.

Want to mingle with the trendy crowd? The **Taste of Randolph Street** (Randolph Street corridor near the intersection of Halsted Street, 773-472-9046) brings together several chichi West Loop Randolph Street restaurants, a vintage auto and motorcycle show, and live music. The **Old Saint Pat's World's Largest Block Party** (Madison Street and Des Plaines Avenue, 312-648-1021), a two-day blowout in mid-July, always brings in great national pop rock acts. It's also a top spot for singles cruising for a partner. Over the years, more than 65 couples have met at this festival and then later tied the knot. Go figure. Another major party is the **Taste of Lincoln Avenue** fest (North Lincoln Avenue between the 2200 and 2400 block, 773-472-9046). This big bash, which usually transpires around the last weekend in July, presents more than 50 bands on five stages. Last year, more than 40 restaurants were represented by booths selling chow, along with another 80 street vendors and a block-long kids' carnival.

If you are to believe some PR person's prattle, then **Around the Coyote** (773-342-6777) is the largest studio walk and art exhibition in the world, gathering close to 1,000 artists. It also features fiction and poetry readings, theatrical performances, and film. It's held for

10 days in mid-September in the Wicker Park/Bucktown neighborhood (roughly around Milwaukee Avenue at North Avenue and Damen Avenue), and there's no doubt this thing is huge. The **Chicago Gospel Fest** (Grant Park), held in early to mid-June in Grant Park, is a three-day event that attracts national, international, and local gospel acts performing on three stages. Between us, this festival can be better than a bottle of Prozac. At any given moment, the entire crowd can erupt, singing a gospel song in unison.

SECRET
STRINGED
INSTRUMENTS

While Chicago is definitely a melting pot of ethnic diversity, **Different Strummer** (4544 North Lincoln Avenue, 773-728-6000, ext. 3) takes this notion to extremes. You're bound to find a sizable selection of traditional stringed instruments like guitars, banjos, mandolins, and dobros. But you will also discover Russian balalaikas, Indian sitars, African koras, and Yugoslavian tamburitzas.

If all you want to do is plug it in and turn it up, the **Guitar Center** (2633 North Halsted Street, 773-327-5687) is the right place to do it. While I find this national chain to be a bit annoying, with its profusion of Eddie Van Halen wannabes noodling away at loud volumes, there's no better selection of electric guitars and basses in Chicago. The store has an ample supply of amplifiers, keyboards, drum kits, effects pedals, and music books.

Real pros go to **Make'ɴ Music** (250 North Artesian Avenue, 312-455-1970). For years, this outfit was located in a desolate industrial corridor with no walk-in business whatsoever. In order to get past the security door, you had to be buzzed in. Today, the place has moved and is proudly, the owners will tell you, in an even more remote location. Make'ɴ Music doesn't live or die on walk-in business. The place is always packed with customers. How do they do it? Reputation. When the Stones come to town, this is where they go. Lenny Kravitz? Ditto. Buddy Guy, Tom Petty...

SECRET
SUNDAY BRUNCH

The **Hotel Florence** (11111 South Forrestville Street, 773-785-8900) makes a lovely brunch: omelettes and eggs and pancakes, oh my! And history buffs will love the old building, built in 1881 by rail-car manufacturer George Pullman. The second story of this hotel, open to the public, showcases several rooms and suites with their original furnishings. **Ann Sather's Restaurant** has two locations (5207 North Clark Street, 773-271-6677; 929 West Belmont Avenue, 773-348-2378) and a delightful, affordable brunch. The gooey, cinnamon-dusted pastries are incredible.

I could eat spicy for breakfast, lunch, and dinner. When I have a hankering for hot on a Sunday, I drop in at **Flo** (1434 West Chicago Avenue, 312-243-0477). The breakfast burritos are loaded with zingy poblano peppers, red onions, salsa, cheddar cheese, and sour cream. If banana cashew flapjacks make your Sunday morning mouth water,

then mosey into the **Bongo Room** (1470 North Milwaukee Avenue, 773-489-0690). You won't be disappointed. Another one of my favorite brunch spots (technically lunch, 'cause it opens at noon, but you should sleep in on Sunday mornings) is **Thai Classic** (3332 North Clark Street, 773-404-2000), where $9.95 buys you an amazing all-you-can-eat Thai buffet of spring rolls, pad Thai, and chicken satay. Take your shoes off, sit cross-legged on the floor, and enjoy.

If you're looking to shell out a wad of cash on a morning meal of pure decadence, go no further than the **Drake Hotel** (140 East Walton Street, 312-787-2200). Served in the **Oak Terrace Room**, the Drake's brunch is a full buffet with omelette and carving stations, and fresh orange juice and bubbly champagne. Of course, you should bring your Visa, because it's $37.50 for adults and $17.50 for kids 6 to 12. Reservations are required. You can find another lavish, splendid buffet at the **Dining Room** at the **Ritz-Carlton Chicago Hotel** (160 East Pearson Street, 312-266-2343). This Sunday-only spread includes made-to-order omelettes, a waffle station, and roasted beef tenderloin. There's fresh seafood like crab and shrimp. This mother-of-all-buffets comes at a price, though: $51 per person.

For something equally upscale minus the price, **Brett's** (2011 West Roscoe Street, 773-248-0999) is a white-tablecloth restaurant on a humble North Side street. For $6.75, you can sup on poached eggs in Creole sauce laid on a bed of black beans. Try the mimosas — a perfect blend of champagne and OJ. **Schuba's** (3159 North Southport Avenue, 773-525-2508) is a Jekyll and Hyde–style establishment. By night, this is one of the best venues in the city for alternative country music. (What's alt country? Traditional country music, six-string acoustic guitars, upright bass, a simple drum kit, and a good measure of Hank Williams Sr.'s inspiration. Go figure, alternative is traditional. In case you can't tell, I hate that pop with a twang crap that passes for country these days. But I digress.) On Sunday mornings, Schuba's dance floor becomes a warm and rustic spot for brunch. The bloody Marys and the mimosas are ample and strong, and the Texas-style French toast is thick and tasty and drenched in sweet, natural maple syrup.

Want some inspiration with your meal? **House of Blues** (329 North Dearborn Street, 312-527-BLUE) has a swingin' Sunday gospel brunch with a southern buffet of biscuits and gravy, cheese grits, jambalaya, and out-of-the-oven-and-onto-your-plate cornbread. Meanwhile, local gospel acts raise a ruckus on the small stage with upbeat, toe-tappin' live music.

S E C R E T
SURGERY
❧

Hidden inside an old four-story mansion along Lake Shore Drive is the **International Museum of Surgical Science** (1524 North Lake Shore Drive, 312-642-6502, www.imss.org). This vast building is dedicated to the macabre history of medical sciences. Covering over 4,000 years of surgery, this often-overlooked museum is the only place in town where you'll find people staring at photographic exhibits of tumors as if they're looking at a Monet painting. In the Hall of the Immortals, a dozen eight-foot statues of great medical heroes, such as Hippocrates and Louis Pasteur, line the room. You'll stumble upon a re-creation of a turn-of-the-century doctor's office, with shelves of rare medical tomes and even postoperative skulls behind glass. Throughout the museum, there's a plethora of tools of the trade:

tooth pliers, prongs, probes, squeezers, calipers, and tweezers. The suggested donation is $5 for adults, $3 for kids and seniors.

S E C R E T
SUSHI

❧

In the mood for sushi? At lunchtime, **Shiroi Hana** (3242 North Clark Street, 773-477-1652) serves a fantastic lunch box that includes nine different sushis and a piping-hot bowl of miso soup for the low price of $7.95. But don't come expecting some sort of minimalist, exposed steel decor imbued with dramatic neon lighting. Shiroi Hana is less about trendy raw bar atmosphere and more about reasonably priced, good sushi.

Okay, so you want that hipster atmosphere and excellent sushi at the same time? No problem. **Mirai** (2020 West Division Street, 773-862-8500) is a favorite with scenesters and late-night loungers. The sushi is also top tier. Along with the stark, monochromatic color scheme, the track lighting, and all the cool, fruity cocktails mixed at the bar, this popular restaurant serves some of the best sushi in Chicago. Delectables include a smoky unagi (cooked freshwater eel) and seared black and white sesame seed–encrusted tuna.

The menu at **Kamehachi** (1400 North Wells Street, 312-664-3663) is enormous, showcasing a mix of maki and delicious combination rolls. The Chicago crazy roll, for example, is a memorable combination of the freshest tuna, salmon, and yellowtail. And while the lines in the happening restaurant can be long, don't despair. The dark upstairs lounge is the perfect spot to wait for that impending wasabi buzz.

And one more place that I am sure you will leave saying "Domo Arigato, Mr. Roboto" to me for recommending to you is **Akai Hana** (3223 Lake Avenue, Wilmette, 847-251-0384). This out of the way restaurant in north suburban Wilmette is a real-deal sushi bar, a spectacular yet straightforward Japanese restaurant. The menu here is extensive, jammed with all sorts of classic sushi, sashimi, and maki. The salmon teriyaki California is a must, presented in a bento box with shrimp, tuna, and salmon sushi.

SECRET
TATTOOS

Whether you've always fantasized about tattooing a tiny butterfly on your ass, or going all out and becoming the modern-day incarnation of Ray Bradbury's fictional Illustrated Man, you can get it done the right way in Chicago. The secret to a good tattoo is a masterful tattoo artist. Here's where to go. **Chicago Tattooing Company** (922 West Belmont Avenue, 773-528-6969) is a classic tattoo parlor with barber chairs for the patrons and haggard artists puffing on smokes between epidermal creations. The shop is encrusted on a city block of hipster havens: sex emporiums, leather stores, incense vendors, and vintage shops. The elevated train roars past just a short distance away. With meticulous patience, the artists will work from the thousands of designs in the display books on the counter, or copy one of your own designs. **Deluxe Tattoo** (1459 West Irving Park Road, 773-549-1594) is another popular parlor, recognized the world over for its detail and vibrant colors. Don't go asking the artists to needle the name of your lover or your mother onto your skin, however. They'd rather not. What if you get dumped or, worse yet, your mom grounds you for getting a tattoo? The staff prefers creating original designs in collaboration with the customers, so it's best to come in with something in mind. At **No Hope No Fear** (1579 North Milwaukee Avenue, 773-772-1960), the artists are the mega-talented James and Tim Kern — identical twins. The Kern brothers both hold bachelor's degrees in fine arts, and they specialize in custom tattoos. They'd rather not work from the same old designs. Have an idea? They'll draw it up to your specifications and deliver anything from a tiny tattoo for $50 to a 30-hour, half-of-your-body creation for $4,000.

SECRET
THEATER

It's no secret in the theater business that serious actors from across the country flock to Chicago for a chance to see their name in lights. Chicago is an A-1 theater town. At last count, there were more than 150 companies staging shows in the city. The biggest and the best, are, of course, the **Steppenwolf Theatre Company** (1650 North Halsted Street, 312-335-1650) and the **Goodman Theatre** (170 North Dearborn Street, 312-443-3800). These two companies stage some of the very best productions in the country — with some of the biggest names. Steppenwolf's founders are a who's who of Hollywood: John Malkovich, Gary Sinise, John Mahoney, Joan Allen. All of the Steppenwolf's founding ensemble comes back regularly to act and direct shows. This is fabulous dramatic theater, well crafted, impeccably

acted. The Goodman draws in big names, too, staging thought-provoking productions with amazing set designs. Both the Steppenwolf and the Goodman have smaller studio spaces that stage even more cutting-edge productions. By all means, if you appreciate theater at all — go!

Fans of the classics will love the **Court Theatre** (5535 South Ellis Avenue, 773-753-4472) on the University of Chicago campus. This company takes its Shakespeare and Chekhov very seriously. This is highbrow stuff. After that, if your cup still hasn't runneth over, explore **Chicago Shakespeare Theater** (600 East Grand Avenue, 312-595-5600), which has really posh new digs on Navy Pier. This is Chicago's only professional theater entirely devoted to the Bard. The new 525-seat theater space was inspired by the Swan Theatre in England's Stratford-upon-Avon and cost upwards of $23 million to construct. There's a garden and even an English pub for post-show relaxation.

Victory Gardens (2257 North Lincoln Avenue, 773-871-3000) is dedicated to producing only work written by local playwrights. The space here is small and intimate, but very professional and wonderfully creative. This is quality theater.

The late-night cult phenomenon *Too Much Light Makes a Baby Go Blind* is always worth checking out at **Neo-Futurarium** (5153 North Ashland Avenue, 773-275-5255). The curtain first opened for this show all the way back in 1989 and the crowds are still wall to wall. Here you'll find a one-hour whirlwind of 30 two-minute plays. The lineup of stories changes all the time with the help of audience participation. This far North Side theater space, which is above a funeral parlor, also stages original shows throughout the year that are consistently good.

But the most inspiring theater in Chicago is often found in the tiny houses scattered across the city in small storefronts, old churches, and fledgling theatrical spaces. This is where struggling actors and green-horn production folks earn their stripes. Many of these companies are itinerant, moving from storefront to storefront, hopscotching around with each production, depending on what stage is available for rent. Check out the *Chicago Reader* or *New City* for up-to-date listings (see "Secret Periodicals").

If sex, drugs, and rock 'n' roll offend you, then the **Defiant Theatre** (312-409-0585), with all of its raw and raunchy bombast, is probably not for you. Otherwise, prepare to be entertained. When this group loses its haughty artistic pretensions, it's like buckshot from a double-barreled shotgun — it can't miss. Learn more about this rule-bending company, now in its seventh season, at www.art-wpag.com/Defiant/home.html.

Puppetry is enjoying a resurgence in popularity, but **Redmoon Theatre** (773-388-9031, www.redmoon.org) is way ahead of the curve. Chicago's most unique theatrical experience awaits you with a visit to this 13-year-old itinerant group, known city-wide for its inventive puppetry and spectacle performances that incorporate all sorts of circus flash, like fire breathing, baton twirling, and stilt walking. Heady and macabre adaptations of *Frankenstein* and *Moby Dick* have received rave reviews. Integrating string-based, rod-based, and larger-than-life puppets manipulated by multiple actors makes for one night of theater you won't want to miss. Redmoon also runs a very active community outreach program, bringing its brand of supercharged creativity to the streets free of charge. If you happen to be trick-or-treating in Chicago, watch for the annual "All Hallows Eve Celebration," which explodes with color, percussion, costumes, puppetry, and fire.

Another very worthy itinerant theater company to watch for is **Lookingglass Theatre** (773-477-9257). And while David Schwimmer of "Friends" fame is a founding member of the group, don't hold that against them. Just a little joke — I'm not a fan of the TV show. The productions here are outstanding. Comprising Northwestern University graduates, this thoughtful company has garnered several Joseph Jefferson Citations, the Academy Awards of Chicago theater.

S E C R E T

TOLL BOOTHS

Disclaimer time. The author of this fine little tome and its publisher, the esteemed ECW Press, are not recommending you try anything illegal. But this book is about secrets, after all, and we would be remiss in not telling you how to, er, shortchange the annoying toll-booths dotting the expressways around Chicagoland. At 40, 50, and even 75 cents a pop, they add up quick. Even worse, the toll authority assured Illinois citizens in 1947 that once the bonds to build the toll roads were paid, the tolls would be taken away. Lies, lies, lies. Today, Illinois drivers still line up and toss money into baskets on roads that have long been paid off. That being the case, you wouldn't feel guilty if I let you in on a dirty little secret to save you the expense of the tolls now, would you? I didn't think so. Okay, then.

The secret can be traced all the way to Cambridge, Massachusetts, and the New England Confectionery Company. Ever hear of NECCO Wafers? They're great little sugary sweets that come in eight pastel-colored flavors. The company that manufactures these little confectionery morsels is more than 150 years old. Currently, 4 billion NECCO Wafers are sold each year. And, oh yeah, they're almost the exact size of quarters. Even better, two wafers and a nickel (for weight) work just fine in the Illinois toll booths — the automatic gates, mind you, not the booths with human beings standing watch. Be discreet. Big brother watches some tollways via videotape.

Since the first edition of this book came out, the Illinois big shots have really been clamping down. If you'd rather not break the law, then why not send a message? The toll authority hates pennies. They fill the machines up too fast. That said . . . use pennies! They don't take long to gather and count and they really piss off the authorities. But if you really want to go with the NECCOS, don't be afraid. Rumor has it that Illinois has had so much trouble with the little quarter-shaped candies that they asked the NECCO company to change the size of their sweets. I bet you can guess where NECCO told the Land o' Lincoln to stick its candy.

S E C R E T
TOYS

❧

I love toys. And truth be told, when I'm all alone, I still take out a GI Joe every now and then and play. It's too bad that adults are culturally forbidden from playing house with Barbies or having high-speed chases on the sofa with Matchbox cars. The world would undoubtedly be a better, gentler, more imaginative place.

Remember the scene in the movie *Big* when Tom Hanks runs across the gigantic floor piano at **F.A.O. Schwarz**? Well, so what if that takes place in the New York store? Chicago has one, too (840 North Michigan Avenue, 312-587-5000). From the toy soldier outside that greets you (and shoots you with a water pistol on hot summer days) to the immense array of gizmos, gadgets, and playthings piled inside, this is every child's fantasy room. The first floor houses stuffed animals and a complete Barbie room; the second floor has the afore-mentioned piano, as well as toddler and tyke goodies like Hello Kitty and Paddington Bear; and the third floor is a stomping ground for sci-fi, action, and nature fans.

At **Quake Collectibles** (4628 North Lincoln Avenue, 773-878-4288), one of the coolest stores around for a Gen-xer, every toy comes from the '60s, '70s, or '80s, a time when Saturday morning cartoons and bowls of sugary cereal were king. You'll find *Planet of the Apes* dolls still in the packages, loads of metal lunch boxes, and even an unopened box of 25-year-old Quake cereal, from which the store takes its name.

If ever a store's name summed up what it was all about, that would be **Uncle Fun** (1338 West Belmont Avenue, 773-477-8223). This charming toy store stocks thousands of little goodies — super balls, magnets, stickers, tin robots, magic tricks, puppets . . . you name it. Most of the toys here have a retro vibe to them, like the toys your fun uncle used to play with when he was a kid. This is a wildly imaginative shop. Don't pass it by.

Sweet Pea (3338 North Southport Avenue, 773-281-4426), a closet-sized shop, stocks toys from around the world: cute wooden cars and classic teddy bears. And if you're of the anti-Sony PlayStation mindset, **Zany Brainy** (2163 North Clybourn Avenue, 773-281-2371) is a wonderful toy store that doesn't pander to attention-deficit kids. Nothing in the store falls under the violent category. What the shop does have is a cornucopia of junior science labs, dinosaur model kits, rock crystal–growing gardens, model trains, kiddie sing-along vid-eos, and other imaginative stuff. Plus, during the holiday season, the shop is way PC. What other toy store offers both Christmas and

Hanukkah gift wrapping for free? **Saturday's Child** (2146 North Halsted Street, 773-525-8697) is a busy shop, packed full of plastic toy animals, super balls, games, model kits, and children's books. This is another shop that emphasizes the imagination, not violence. Do you see a trend here?

SECRET
TRATTORIAS

I'm not much for the new "gourmet" Italian trend — hefty price tags and tiny portions. I'm more inclined to frequent an establishment where the owner still cooks in the kitchen and yells out, "Orders up!" I don't want to valet-park my car. I don't want to wait in the piano bar for two hours before getting a table. I don't want to swirl my wine in the glass and chew on it. And I don't want to pay $20 for angel-hair pasta.

At **Ambrogio** (6706 West Belmont Avenue, 773-736-6131), the sign outside announces that they cater funerals. Now we're talking. If the neighborhood trusts them to set up a chafing dish of rigatoni at Grandma's funeral, they've got to be good. Right? Right. This is a true neighborhood joint, in every sense of the word. The small dining room is dark and inviting. The waitresses tell you about their grown kids. The food is heavy and rich in an enticing red sauce, served in generous portions. It's like eating over at the house of someone's Italian uncle.

If ever a meal was worth a 45-minute drive, it would be at **Luigi's** (1315 Sarana Avenue, 630-293-5300). Housed in an old service station in the suburb of West Chicago, the restaurant has only eight or ten tables. This comfortable place is so small you can watch the owner in the kitchen make each and every dish. Everything on the menu is mouth-wateringly good and a couple can leave with a tab in the $20 range. My recommendation: the gnocchi. The meatballs are exquisite. And, oh yes, it's a BYOB establishment. But they'll supply the plastic cups.

Tufano's Vernon Park Tap (1073 West Vernon Park Place, 312-733-3393) is a family-run restaurant just on the edge of the Little Italy neighborhood. Sure, this area is loaded with lots of ultra-expensive alternatives, but why would you waste the money when Tufano's serves up hearty red-sauced dishes in the $7 to $13 range? It's been here 60 years. That says something. And so does the wall of photos of celebrities who have wined and dined here. Dolly Parton really knows her Italian. It's loud and a bit boisterous, but that's what makes it fun. If you are looking for something a bit more romantic, **Bruna's Ristorante** (2424 South Oakley Avenue, 773-254-5550) has been making diners happy since 1933. The lighting is dim and the owner is a first-generation Italian from Tuscany. Well-chosen wine, too!

Waxing more upscale, **Trattoria Dinotto** (163 West North Avenue, 312-787-3345) is a chic eatery with quite possibly the most superb risotto to be found anywhere in Chicago. Start with the grilled calamari and the rosemary bread and this lovely, romantic one-room restaurant will become a favorite. Another great date restaurant is **Rose Angelis** (1314 West Wrightwood Avenue, 773-296-0081), a warm and friendly house on a quiet neighborhood street. Great wine. Even better bruschetta. The restaurant shines with its vegetarian selection.

Coco Pazzo (300 West Hubbard Street, 312-836-0900), no question, falls into that ritzy-glitzy realm. This downtown establishment is by no means a "neighborhood joint," but with its Tuscan charm and delightful menu, it's worth wading through the throngs of fur coat–clad patrons for a wonderful meal.

S E C R E T
24-HOUR DINING

When it comes to all-night establishments, admittedly, Chicago plays second city to New York. While the Big Apple is "the city that never sleeps," the Windy City likes to tuck in at around 2 AM. So where do you go if you want a bite to eat or you have business to take care of in the wee hours? There are a few choice spots — you just have to look around.

The **Golden Apple**, with several locations in Chicago, is open 24–7. It offers classic American coffee shop fare, including round-the-clock breakfast chow. The **Pick Me Up** café (3408 North Clark Street, 773-248-6613) stays open until 3 AM on weeknights and 24 hours on weekends. This little nook is a favorite of the coffeehouse crowd cramming for a big test or suffering from insomnia due to caffeine jitters. The Italian sandwiches are thick and the vegetarian chili, with hulking slices of honey wheat bread, is delightfully piping hot.

A favorite of the inebriate set is **El Presidente** (2558 North Ashland Avenue, 773-525-7938), a Mexican dive that never, ever closes. It's nothing fancy, just good cheap Mexican fare. And when you're blasted at 5 AM, does it really matter how great the food is? Another real treasure is **Lawrence Fisheries** (2120 South Canal Street, 312-225-2113). Nestled between Chinatown and the Pilsen neighborhood, this all-night establishment has a menu that includes scrumptious fried catfish, popcorn shrimp, and seafood gumbo, among other goodies. This roadside joint is like a lonely interstate truck stop dropped in the middle of the urban jungle. When the witching hour sets in, big rigs idle outside by the Chicago River, while road-weary drivers dine inside the restaurant.

For truly legendary Polish sausage (another Chicago favorite), you won't do much better than the **Maxwell Street Depot** (411 West 31st Street, 312-326-3514). It stays open all night, every night. A favorite with the theater community is the **Melrose Restaurant** (3233 North Broadway Street, 773-327-2060), where the selection of 20 different omelettes, 24 hours a day, 7 days a week, is a big hit.

Red eye travelers will praise the 24–7 **Brandy's Restaurant** (5200 South Cicero Avenue, 773-767-0400) for its proximity to Midway Airport and its splendid coffee shop fare. Here, your coffee cup will never go empty. How can you go wrong?

And if you really need a kick, a real wake-up, try **Korean Restaurant** (2659 West Lawrence Avenue, 773-878-2095), where the soups are fiery and the fried mandu is lethally spicy.

SECRET
UFOs

✿

Very few people know that one of the world's preeminent research facilities on unidentified flying objects is in Chicago. **The J. Allen Hynek Center for UFO Studies** (2457 West Peterson Avenue, 773-271-3611, www.cufos.org) was founded in 1973 by — you guessed it —

J. Allen Hynek, a professor of astronomy at Northwestern University in Evanston, Illinois. Hynek, a former science consultant for the us Air Force's inquiry into extraterrestrial sightings, started the center after completing his tenure with Uncle Sam. He has since passed away, but the center carries on the mission to document sightings and to serve as a research facility for anyone interested in little green men. There are more than 50,000 reports of saucer sightings and alien abductions on file. Ironically, there have been no famous visits by creatures from outer space to Chicago. Why? Perhaps it's the invisible cloud of bratwurst steam that looms over the city, acting as a defense shield. Or as the center explains it, no American metropolis is a hotbed for ufo reports. According to research, hicks in the sticks have cornered the market on flying saucer sightings. The Hynek Center is a nonprofit organization that sustains itself by publishing a journal on ufo studies. You can subscribe to the quarterly magazine for $25 on the organization's Web site. If you're interested in visiting the Hynek office, contact them first.

SECRET

USED BOOKS

I love used bookstores and their shelves groaning under the weight of dusty books. The stores smell of old pages, time-tattered covers, and printer's ink. I love that books are cheap and that I can find titles long out of print.

One of my favorite places in Chicago is the **Bookworks** (3444 North Clark Street, 773-871-5318). It's warm and esoteric and a great place to visit after dining at one of the many excellent restaurants in the Lakeview neighborhood. The Bookworks has a tremendous selection of fiction and nonfiction, literary criticism, science fiction, and arts and entertainment material. And it sells old vinyl records.

For an overwhelming selection in a store that stays open late (doors close at 1 AM Monday through Saturday), try **Myopic Books** (1468 North Milwaukee Avenue, 773-862-4882). This vast, cluttered two-story shop is in the center of the trendy, artsy Wicker Park neighborhood.

While **Bookman's Corner** (2959 North Clark Street, 773-929-8298) is a bit of a crazed, unorganized mess, there's something magical about the shop. Books are scattered and stacked all over the place, and you never know what you might find. The **Gallery Bookstore** (3827 North Broadway Street, 773-975-8200) is a tiny little space, but well organized and well stocked. **Afterwords New & Used Books** (23 East Illinois Street, 312-464-1110) stocks both hard to find books and brand new bestsellers.

While it's almost a crime to call **Printers Row Fine & Rare Books** (715 South Dearborn Street, 312-583-1800) a used bookstore, technically, that's what it is — a very high-end used bookstore. This charming shop is located in the historic Printers Row District, in the building where the first edition of *The Wonderful Wizard of Oz* was printed. Store owner Doug Phillips has created a stunning bookshop designed to evoke a Victorian feel. Phillips calls it a "brand new 100-year-old bookstore." The store has leaded glass cabinetry, a fireplace mantel from a century-old funeral home, and an oak bookcase found in an old English pub. On any given day, the store might have a second Shakespeare Folio, first printed in 1632 and priced at $100,000. There are nearly 8,000 books, mostly first editions. Many are signed, by authors ranging from Nathaniel Hawthorne to my own literary god, Ray Bradbury.

SECRET
VEGETARIAN

While Chicago certainly has a reputation as the city of meat eaters, vegetarians can find a home here, too. In the Rogers Park neighborhood, right off the Red Line (Morse stop), sits the **Heartland Café** (7000 North Glenwood Avenue, 773-465-8005). This august little eatery almost belongs on Telegraph Avenue in Berkeley circa the summer of love. It's just a small house in the middle of a tree-shrouded neighborhood street. The cozy front porch is screened in, like an old country house, and is a perfect spot for dining. The café offers an incredible lineup of community events, political rallies, and live music. And the food is pure earthy ecstasy. There is a bounty of creative tofu and tempeh dishes, along with splendid soups and salads. There are plenty of meat dishes on the menu, too. My recommendation: the vegetarian chili and a big wedge of cornbread.

"Meat free since '83" is the motto at the **Chicago Diner** (3411 North Halsted Street, 773-935-6696). The inventive eatery creates all sorts of entrées made with meat substitutes. The seitan fajitas — prepared with whole wheat — are popular and more than palatable to even the most ardent meat lover. The portobello mushroom sandwich is another favorite with the veggie/vegan crowd. The future burger, a grain patty with a side of couscous, is a safe but mouthwatering choice for the non-vegetarian.

While it's in no way a vegetarian restaurant, for salad lovers, the very best salad bar in all of Chicago can be found at **RJ Grunts** (2056 North Lincoln Park West, 773-929-5363). Though not a huge spread, the food at the bar is good and remarkably fresh. Parking in this neighborhood is a crapshoot, so be patient.

SECRET
VIETNAMESE

I've got the inside skinny on this one. My wife is 100-percent Viet-namese. She was born in the far southern town of Can Tho, Vietnam, and she knows her native cuisine like nobody's business. And you know what? The majority of travel guides to Chicago have got it all wrong. They either rattle off a quick list of mediocre Vietnamese eateries or push the swanky French-influenced establishments.

The simple rule of thumb, with any ethnic cuisine, is to go where the locals go. For Vietnamese dining, this would be Uptown. But don't be mistaken by the misnomer New Chinatown that people are throwing around these days in reference to this area. The Uptown neighborhood is more like a Little Saigon. The El stop at Argyle puts you right in the heart of this Vietnamese neighborhood. From the El platform, where the jade green pagoda beckons you to peer down onto Argyle Street, you can inhale the aroma of roasted duck, seen hanging upside down in storefronts, and watch shoppers bump into each other as they wander from shoe stores to foreign video stores to grocer's stands. While it lacks the gentrified sheen of, say, Lincoln Park, Lakeview, or Wicker Park, Uptown is real Chicago: it's unpolished and it bustles. Most of that activity surrounds the numerous Vietnamese restaurants.

Vietnamese cuisine is neither Chinese's poorer cousin nor Thai's step-sister. It's lighter and more tropical. When you go out for a quintes-sentially Vietnamese meal like pho (a steaming bowl of noodle soup), you should be on the lookout for a side dish of fresh jalapeños, bean sprouts, mint basil, saw-leaf herbs, and lime wedges, all of which you heap on top of your bowl of pho. But how do you pick the best place for pho? In any good Vietnamese neighborhood, a pho house exists. Uptown's best is **Pho Hoa** (4929 North Broadway Street, 773-784-8723). The menu guides the novice to beginner's fare like eye of round steak noodle soup, and to the more maverick tripe soup. In total, there are 17 variations of the meal, which is served for breakfast, lunch, and dinner. Your meal will arrive on your table mere minutes after you order, but don't expect attentive service. It's normal; the restaurant draws a local crowd that doesn't expect such service, so don't stand out and demand it. To fit in even more, sip on the beverage of choice, cafe sua da, or iced coffee.

My wife and I stumbled upon **Dong Ky** (4877 North Broadway Street, 773-989-5579) when we were in the mood for Vietnamese but didn't want to deal with the crazy parking in the Tai Nam shopping center where Pho Hoa is located. So we went out on a limb and tried Dong Ky, a hole in the wall a few blocks away. We were skeptical at first, but the food here is ridiculously cheap and gratifyingly delicious. For spring rolls (the appetizer), a tofu crepe (entrée), and jackfruit shake (dessert), we spent a little over $10. There are 147 items on the menu — everything from fried taro-root cake, and Dungeness crab stir-fried with ginger and curried tofu, to stuffed steamed rice crepes. And Dong Ky also has pho!

But what's the best Vietnamese food? Food you prepare. Vietnamese food takes hours to put together, when done right. To make pho, you need to simmer the broth for a good hour, and that's just the beginning. The whole process, when my mother-in-law does it, goes on for a solid three to four hours. And this, of course, is half the fun. The family gathers in the kitchen, and each person is assigned a task: one cuts the beef sirloin into paper-thin slices, another washes the various herbs and sprouts, while yet another boils the rice noodles, all the while laughing, bickering, and bantering. You won't experience this in any restaurant. Start at the **Tai Nam Supermarket** (4925 North Broadway Street, 773-275-5666) to get your ingredients. This store is a hectic, cramped market, well stocked with 25-pound bags of rice, exotic produce, and aisles of powdered curry, chili, and tamarind. And it's far cheaper than the chain supermarkets. Another excellent Asian market that supplies ingredients you won't find in standard American grocery stores — such as canned sugar cane and fresh bamboo sprouts — is **Broadway Supermarket** (4879 North Broadway Street, 773-334-3838).

All right, we will acquiesce on one thing. **Le Colonial** (937 North Rush Street, 312-255-0088), a froufrou French-Vietnamese restaurant in the uppity Gold Coast district, has great atmosphere. While other, corporate travel guides will sing the praises of the overpriced and underportioned mediocre food, the real reasons to come here are the balcony and the bar. The bar is dark, with fans lazily whipping overhead, and luxurious sofas lit all around with votive candles. It's Saigon during the 1920s French occupation, if you like that kind of colonial bullshit.

S E C R E T
VINTAGE

I have spent long autumn days hopscotching from one vintage shop to the next, looking for that perfect bowling shirt or that perfect Eisenhower-era suit or that sterling silver tie bar just like the one Grandpa used to wear. And I suppose my biggest obsessions are vintage Hawaiian shirts. There's just something about vintage shopping that's so much more rewarding than a trek to the local mall. It's the hunt. The quest to find buried treasure amidst a heap of trash. Chicago has an abundance of vintage shops with all sorts of hidden surprises.

A great place to start your vintage shopping spree is in Boystown, the area where a large percentage of the gay community resides (for more on this neighborhood, see "Secret Boystown"). Start at **Flashy Trash** (3524 North Halsted Street, 773-327-6900) and work your way south. Keep in mind, however, that this first stop may be one of the best. Flashy Trash specializes in very well-cared-for men's and women's clothing, hats, and accessories. You can buy a mint-condition baby-blue polyester tuxedo with matching ruffled shirt, or you can pick up a 1940s fedora that looks like it just came from the haberdasher.

If you wander farther south down Halsted, **Beatnix** (3400 North Halsted Street, 773-281-6933) is loaded with retro clothes, worn leather jackets, ratty faux furs, utility shirts, ties, and jewelry. Plus, the window displays here are a hoot. The shopkeepers have continually pushed the envelope with all sorts of male mannequins dressed up as cowboys and Chicago cops contorted and propped in racy, sexual positions. Some neighbors have complained, and the local alderman's office has even asked the shop to remove the risqué presentations. Beatnix always complies and then replaces the exhibits with something equally offensive to the prudes.

One more notable Boystown vintage shop is the **Silver Moon** (3337 North Halsted Street, 773-883-0222). You won't find bell bottoms or platform shoes here. Instead, you'll score more upscale threads from the 1890s through the 1960s. Silver Moon specializes in resale wedding gowns and suits for hipsters in the nouveaux-swing movement.

Next up is the massive **Hollywood Mirror** (812 West Belmont Avenue, 773-404-4510), which carries an overwhelming array of vintage clothes organized by style, size, and color. There's also a basement loaded with furniture and housewares. There are '50s-era dinette tables, and lamps and chairs straight from a 1970s bachelor pad. On the second floor, above Hollywood Mirror, is **Ragstock** (773-868-9263). This is another warehouse-sized emporium of used clothing. I usually find great work shirts here with other people's names stitched above the breast pocket. It really confuses some people when I introduce myself and my shirt says "Paul." Ragstock is jammed with old corduroy pants, blue jeans, sweaters, suits, dresses, and really neat Japanese baseball jerseys. Incidentally, it carries new clothing as well.

Hubba Hubba (3309 North Clark Street, 773-477-1414) is an upscale boutique offering new and vintage women's clothing with a romantic Victorian bent. The smell of lavender potpourri is omnipresent. Flowers and pearls and lace are everywhere. You'll find a wonderful selection of one-of-a-kind jewelry and accessories, including gloves and silk scarves and eyeglass frames. **Strange Cargo** (3448 North Clark Street, 773-327-8090) returns you to the realm of cheap retro, circa the '50s through '80s. It also has a good selection of used Levi's and my footwear of choice, Converse Chuck Taylor All-Stars.

Just about 5 or 10 minutes away by foot, along the very trendy Southport corridor, **Wisteria** (3715 North Southport Avenue, 773-880-5868) is a hep cat's haven. It's on the pricey side, since everything here is in really fine condition, but you'll score pristine vintage suits and dresses and hear some great old jazz while you shop.

In Wicker Park, you'll find the best selection of vintage leather and suede jackets at US **#1 Vintage Clothing & Denim** (1509 North Milwaukee Avenue, 773-489-9428). It also sells racks and racks of recycled jeans. And one more neat thing about this shop — there are two very gentle, huge dogs that are always lounging about waiting for affection. If you get a chance, tell them that the dog lover who wrote this book said "hi."

S E C R E T
VOYEURISM

So you like to watch, huh? My favorite spy spot is the second-story café within the massive **Borders Books & Music** (830 North Michigan Avenue, 312-573-0564). Stake out a window seat looking down upon the Mag Mile and you'll catch a glimpse of all facets of humanity. The popular horse-and-carriage rides begin here and, in summer, long lines of couples and families wait their turn to be carried Cinderella-like around this marble and glass district. Street musicians bang on plastic buckets, their percussive beats filling the evening air. Businesswomen in power suits and running shoes cross the street with tourists, as cops in busy intersections bark at motorists. All this and you can leave without even buying a book.

It has been said that New York City shops sell more telescopes than anywhere else on Earth. Amazing, considering you can't see a single star in the sky because of all the city light. And while penthouse peeping isn't as popular in Chicago, you can still spot plenty of tripods in high-rise apartment windows. **Central Camera Company** (230 South Wabash Avenue, 312-427-5580) and **Helix Camera & Video** (310 South Racine Avenue, 312-421-6000) both stock numerous telescopes and binoculars powerful enough to view the nose hairs on

a fruit fly. All you have to do now is find a friend living in a high-rise apartment. My recommended location: **Marina City** (300 North State Street), right in the thick of all the downtown action.

But the very best voyeuristic vantage point in the city is aboard the **Howard/Dan Ryan Red Line** elevated train. While many El trains run along seen-one-you've-seen-'em-all expressways, the Red Line glides through the middle of neighborhoods, often right past kitchen windows and back porches. Just a few feet away, you'll peer into the lives of Chicagoans: cooking dinner, talking on the telephone phone, and, yes, I've even seen a nude body or two along the way.

SECRET
WEB CAMS

Web cams are cool offshoots of the dot-com craze. They feed live video footage to the World Wide Web 24 hours a day. Several are positioned around the city, affording anyone with Internet access a chance to peer into Chicago life as it happens. Some of these Web cams show pretty skyline shots. The cam atop the **Field Museum** (www.earthcam.com/usa/illinois/chicago/field/), for example, posts a beautiful live view of the city that rotates in several directions. You can watch traffic moving north on Lake Shore Drive, catch a glimpse of Navy Pier, check out the museum campus and Grant Park, and marvel at the Sears Tower.

But the Field Museum doesn't just offer a live shot from its roof. Navigate to www.fmnh.org/sue/default_icam.htm to peep into the dinosaur fossil lab, which put together the world's largest known

T-Rex, Sue. Here, Web voyeurs can watch museum visitors peering through the lab windows. On heavy traffic days, kids on field trips stand gawking, screwing around, and even picking their noses for the camera. Say cheese.

Visit **www.rreese.com** for another spectacular shot of downtown. The camera is set atop a building in Chicago's glitzy Gold Coast neighborhood. The view looks east at the John Hancock Center and Michigan Avenue. The Web cam set high atop the **Adler Planetarium** (www.adlerplanetarium.org/skyeye/) posts a beautiful live view of the city that allows online users to direct the camera in a 360-degree rotation, zoom, and focus. It's pretty cool.

Loyola University has two Web cams. The first (www.luc.edu/webcam/wtc) broadcasts a live glimpse of the Water Tower Plaza. The second cam (www.luc.edu/webcam/lsc/) is located at the University's Crown Center and it looks south down the shoreline of Lake Michigan. Both shots are quite magnificent.

For several great Web-cam views all connected to one site, the **City of Chicago** offers fascinating, live, and, in some cases, rotatable views of Midway Airport, Navy Pier, and Wacker Drive. Take a look at www.ci.chi.il.us/LiveShots/.

SECRET
WEDDINGS

Justice of the peace wedding ceremonies are usually reserved for shotgun nuptials or for couples disenchanted with the mega-expensive church/reception/limo song-and-dance. But, thanks to the City of

Chicago, quickie civil court weddings are no longer relegated to the glum, fluorescent-lit bowels of City Hall. Every Saturday morning from 9 AM to noon, in beautiful GAR Hall at the **Chicago Cultural Center** (78 East Washington Street, 312-346-3278), lovey-dovey couples can tie the knot with some semblance of class. With the opulent stained-glass dome overhead and a little music from a city-subcontracted DJ, couples can get it over with, without the Martha Stewart shenanigans that drain the father of the bride's bank account. To inquire about this service or to make reservations, call 312-602-5660. By the way, this service is cheap. Ten bucks and you're hitched.

How's this for different: getting married on a CTA elevated train. During normal operation, there's no smoking, littering, or radio playing, but if you book a car for a private bash, you can do whatever you please. For more scoop, call the **Chicago Transit Authority** at 312-664-7200.

But that's not the end of it. You can book plenty of other bizarre/cool/eccentric/goofy locations. How 'bout the **Scholl College of Podiatric Medicine** (1001 North Dearborn Street, 312-280-2909)? Only seven colleges for podiatric medicine exist in the entire US, and you can book one of them for your nuptials. Bunion removal costs extra.

Would-be Dr. Doolittles can get hitched near the animals at the **Lincoln Park Zoo** (2001 North Clark Street, 312-337-3337), where there are beautiful gardens and a petting zoo. Bookish types can always marry on the top floor of the **Harold Washington Public Library** (400 South Street, 312-747-4130) in the glass-ceilinged **Winter Garden**. Seriously, this is one of the most beautiful new interiors added to the Chicago architectural landscape in recent years. For something utterly urban, utterly cool, check out the **HotHouse** (31 East Balbo Avenue, 312-362-9707). This multi-arts center (see

"Secret Jazz") is nestled into a neon-hued pocket of the South Loop and is the perfect artsy, metropolitan setting for a private bash.

One sweet spot is the **South Shore Cultural Center** (7059 South Shore Drive, 312-747-2536), where my wife and I got married. This lavish, turn-of-the-century spread is a former country club planted right on the edge of Lake Michigan on the city's South Side. The center has two grand Art Deco–style banquet rooms available for private parties. We chose the sun-drenched Solarium, which looks straight out upon the shimmering blue waters of Lake Michigan. This place comes highly recommended! For more on this lovely locale, check out "Secret African American."

S E C R E T

WELLNESS

My dad's been on me lately about taking care of myself. A decade of living the writer's life takes its toll. So I've started to investigate the healthy side of living in Chicago, and here are a few places I've discovered that I'll share with you. **Sherwyn's** (645 West Diversey Avenue, 773-477-1934) is the be-all and end-all of health food and vitamin stores. It supplies an impressive amount of whole grains, organic produce, and dairy products, along with shelf after shelf of vitamins from A to, well, zinc.

At the 73-year-old **Dr. Michael's Herb Center** (5109 North Western Avenue, 773-271-7738), you'll discover more than 400 herbs, give or take, depending on the time of year. How about some mullen leaves for that lingering cough? And while Dr. Michael passed on some years ago despite his herbal efforts, his son now runs the shop.

In the heart of the charming Lincoln Square neighborhood on the city's North Side, you'll find an honest-to-goodness, old-fashioned apothecary. **Merz Apothecary** (4750 North Lincoln Avenue, 773-561-3377) carries all sorts of herbal and homeopathic remedies.

Most health nuts are singing the praises of green tea these days. Research suggests that the antioxidants found in the tea neutralize harmful molecules in the body. **Sunflower Seed Health Foods** (5210 South Harper Avenue, 773-363-1600) stocks five different brands of green tea, along with other herbal teas, such as echinacea and chamomile. They also grind their own peanut butter.

For even more good health, the **Lakeview Holistic Center** (1430 West Belmont Avenue, 773-244-5400) handles just about everything. Need a colonic? No problemo. That'll be $75, thank you very much. The duration of the treatment depends on your diet. Acupuncture? You got it. You will also find massage, magnet therapy, aromatherapy, homeopathy, and ear candling, which uses a small candle to relieve pressure in the ear canal.

SECRET
WRITERS' BARS

Literary scholars have long pondered why so many writers drink like there's no tomorrow. And many Chicago scribes could go shot-for-shot with the best of 'em. Native sons Ernest Hemingway and newspaperman Mike Royko were just two Windy City writers with a penchant for pickling their livers. So why do so many writers like to sauce it up? As the beer ad goes, "Why ask why?" The more important question is, "Where do writers like to sauce it up?"

The **Billy Goat Tavern** (430 North Michigan Avenue, 312-222-1525) is a legendary writerly watering hole made famous years ago on "Saturday Night Live." Remember? "Cheezeborger! Cheezeborger! No Pepsi, Coke!" This is the place. Just a short haul from the *Chicago Tribune* offices and the *Sun-Times* building, this is a newspaper bar, packed after hours with staff writers unloading after meeting their deadlines. This was Mike Royko's home away from home. In the good old days when newspapermen were real men, they used to take their arguments out on the street, often coming to fisticuffs on Lower Wacker Drive. Today, most journalists favor Starbucks coffee over beer and they choose to fight through petty pissing matches in their own columns. Still, the Goat has a comforting, old-school edge.

Sterch's (2238 North Lincoln Avenue, 773-281-2653) attracts a score of scribes from publications as diverse as *Playboy, Esquire,* and *Sports Illustrated.* You can also share a cocktail with local television news producers, and even a few nonfiction authors and novelists who call this their tavern of choice. Still, it's definitely a journalist's watering hole. But if you don't smoke, bring an oxygen tank — the circulation in here sucks and the room has a permanent yellowish nicotine tattoo.

On Thursday nights at the **Ten Cat** (3931 North Ashland Avenue, 773-935-5377), writers gather. Journalists, magazine writers, novelists, and short-story scribes flock around the pool table or the cozy fireplace in the back room to talk shop.

But perhaps the best bar for listening to some drunk and disorderly writer tell tall tales is the **Old Town Ale House** (219 West North Avenue, 312-944-7020). This is a true bar's bar: dark, waxy wood paneling, smoke, smoke, and more smoke, and it stays open until 4 AM. This is where the old-school journalists go — the ones with their sleeves rolled up, cigarettes dangling from their lips, and that flinty look in their eyes.

S E C R E T
'ZINES
✤

Fanzines, or *'zines*, as they are referred to by the hipsters who read and produce them, are self-published magazines and books dedicated to all sorts of cool (and oftentimes downright weird) material that bigtime publishers wouldn't go near. The actual origins of 'zines are a bit hazy. Some will tell you that they had their genesis in the 1950s when science fiction fans started publishing journals devoted to their favorite SF authors and filmmakers. Other 'zineologists will insist that fanzines sprouted up as a part of the 1960s counterculture revolution. And then there are those who will maintain that 'zines jolted forth from the punk movement of the 1970s. Whenever 'zines originated, they are undeniably a true alternative art form.

The best place to find 'zines in Chicago is at **Quimby's** (1854 West North Avenue, 773-342-0910). Quimby's is a literary amusement park for adults. And while it operates a Web site (www.quimbys.com), this little shop in the artsy Wicker Park neighborhood must be seen to be believed. Every shelf explodes with fringe frontier and pop culture propaganda. UFOS. Sex. Drugs. Conspiracy theories. Technology. Quimby's has it all — along with some mighty fine underground comic books. It also carries some great material published right in the

Windy City. *Rocktober*, a music 'zine, makes for a cool and informed read. *Sport Literate*, a Chicago-based journal focused on the literary side of the sports and leisure world, is always impressive, boasting some of the best blossoming writers the city has to offer. And, of course, you'll want to check out Chris Ware's hugely popular *Acme Novelty Library* for some mighty fine comic book material. Quimby's is cool. And keep your eyes open: underground comic progenitor Jay Lynch, a contemporary and friend of the infamous R. Crumb, lives close by and shops Quimby's religiously.

Another hot spot for 'zine material is **Chicago Comics** (3244 North Clark Street, 773-528-1983), which boasts a plentiful trove (see "Secret Comic Books"). No surprise: Chicago Comics is owned by Eric Kirsammer, the very same gent who has the deed on Quimby's.

Tower Records/Videos/Books (2301 North Clark Street, 773-477-5994) has an impressive selection, too, not to mention the best music selection in Chicago. And best of all, it's open until midnight.

SECRET FUTURE

No tour guide can be definitively comprehensive, especially when the aim is to uncover those hidden places that have previously escaped notice. Undoubtedly, some worthwhile attractions have remained hidden even from our best efforts to ferret them out.

In the interest of our own self-improvement, we ask readers to let us know of the places they've unearthed that they believe warrant inclusion in future editions of *Secret Chicago*. If we use your suggestion, we'll send you a free copy on publication. Please contact us at the following address:

Secret Chicago
C/O ECW PRESS

2120 Queen Street East, Suite 200
Toronto, Ontario, Canada M4E 1E2

Or e-mail us at: info@secretguides.com

PHOTO SITES

SUBJECT INDEX

Love and Romance

Lunch Spots/Light Meals

Markets and Malls

Sacred Spaces/Hallowed Places

ALPHABETICAL INDEX